The RESCUE Of TIMMY TRIAL

E.M.WILKIE

THE RESCUE OF TIMMY TRIAL

Aletheia Adventure Series Book 1

E M Wilkie

JOHN RITCHIE LTD
CHRISTIAN PUBLICATIONS

40 Beansburn, Kilmarnock, Scotland

ISBN-13: 978 1 909803 55 8

www.ritchiechristianmedia.co.uk

Written by E M Wilkie
Illustrated by E M Wilkie
Copyright © 2013

Cover illustration by Graeme Hewitson.
Interior illustrations are by E M Wilkie.

Unless otherwise indicated, Scripture quotations are taken from:
The Holy Bible, New King James Version®.
© 1982 by Thomas Nelson, Inc. Used by permission. All rights reserved.

To Zach,
This story was written for you.

*"The snare is broken, and we have escaped
Our help is in the name of the Lord..."*

Psalm 124:7

PREFACE

This story is an attempt to help and encourage young readers to develop an understanding of the truth contained in the Word of God, the Bible. However, all characters, places, descriptions and incidents are entirely fictional and this adventure story is not intended to be a substitute for the teaching contained in the Bible, but rather an aid to understanding. The illustrations and allegories used in this story are not perfect; and therefore, whilst it is hoped that readers will benefit from the truth and lessons developed in this story, they must be urged to develop an understanding of Bible truth and doctrine from the Bible alone.

The author would like to acknowledge the invaluable help and advice of the following people in the writing of this book: M J Wilkie, R Hatt, S Mickow, and E Hatt.

Contents

Map Of The City Of Aletheia   8

Map Of The Land Of Err   9

Chapter 1: The Locked Shed   11

Chapter 2: Behind The Door   21

Chapter 3: The Adventure Begins   31

Chapter 4: Into The Unknown   43

Chapter 5: The City Of Aletheia   55

Chapter 6: At Home With The Wallops   67

Chapter 7: A Sound In The Night   79

Chapter 8: Timmy Goes His Own Way   91

Chapter 9: Wishy-Washy Fair   105

Chapter 10: The Prophecies Of Wander Palm   119

Chapter 11: A Night In The Forest   133

Chapter 12: Taken Captive!   147

Chapter 13: The Rescue Craft   159

Chapter 14: The Exploding Drink   171

Chapter 15: Danger! Snares!   189

Chapter 16: Mr Weighty To The Rescue   203

Chapter 17: Back To Aletheia   217

Chapter 18: Home At Last   229

Bible References   239

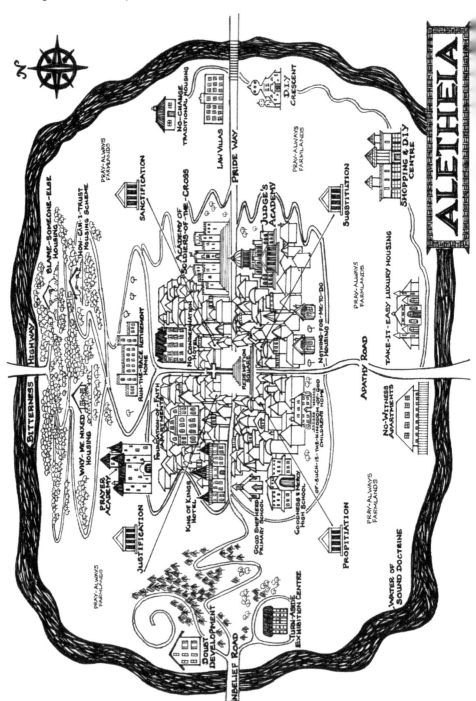

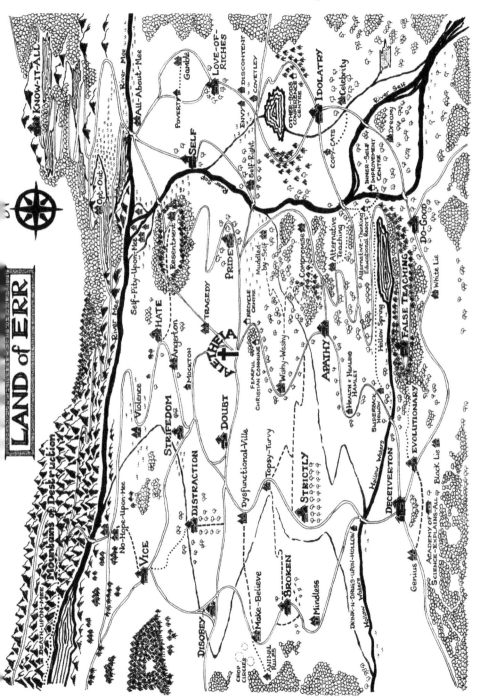

CHAPTER 1
THE LOCKED SHED

Jack Merryweather was an ordinary boy to whom extraordinary things never happened. In fact, Jack had never had a proper adventure in the whole of his life. It wasn't that he didn't want an adventure: Jack wanted one very much. He read about adventures; he dreamed about adventures; he even tried writing his own adventures. Recently Mrs Bubble, his schoolteacher, whom Jack suspected didn't believe in adventures at all, had set an assignment entitled 'Description of Trees in the Summer'. Jack had managed to avoid the main subject of trees in the summer or winter or at any other specified time. Instead he had created an ugly, man-eating tree and a wonderful gory adventure. Mrs Bubble had written the remark *"Excellent imagination for adventures, although not much content about trees"* on the assignment. It was the first time that Jack had received an 'excellent' for anything and he was pleased it was for an adventure. He didn't mind the remark about trees at all; anyone could write about trees; not many people could write a good adventure.

Jack grabbed his spy watch from his bedside table as Mum

once more called up the stairs. "Time for school, Jack," she said. "You really will miss breakfast if you're much longer!"

Jack stuck his spy watch in his pocket. He picked up his school rucksack and stopped only briefly to look out of his bedroom window. This was a habit of his. He liked to imagine that unknown creatures lived in the huge leafy tree outside of the window. He hadn't exactly seen any, but a couple of times he had climbed the tree, right to the top branches, and examined small holes and marks which might mean that *something* lived there. But today he could see no movement to indicate anything remotely unknown; he could only see rays of sunshine shining brightly from a cloudless blue sky, right through the green leaves.

It didn't seem fair to spend such a hot summer day at school when Grandad might be working on his combine harvester today. Grandad had promised Jack that he could help steer the monstrous machine through the fields of wheat and barley, where it gobbled up the grain and stripped everything completely bare. But at least it was Friday.

All of Saturday Jack might sit with Grandad far above the sea of waving stalks, feeling like a king in charge of the world.

And, if he managed it, at lunchtime today he could perhaps sneak away for a moment to the gap in the hedge at the edge of the school, where Grandad's fields and big sheds joined onto the playground. Perhaps Grandad was combining today.

It was day-dreamy kind of weather in the hot, stuffy classroom. The sun streamed through the windows and the teacher, Mrs Bubble, looked hot and cross and bothered. Nearly everyone, apart from Marigold Goody who never did anything wrong, was restless, and two boys had already been sent out of the classroom for bad behaviour. Jack wondered what they were doing and if they had managed to sneak away to the big tree on the playing fields. Perhaps he should get sent out of the classroom too. He tore off a corner of his exercise book, which contained unfinished sums, and scrunched it up nice and small. He considered Marigold Goody's yellow pigtails and bent head. She was a very easy target.

Mrs Bubble, who even when hot and bothered seemed to have several invisible eyes in her head, suddenly materialised behind Jack. "It's nearly lunchtime, Jack," she said. "I don't suppose you would enjoy spending it indoors, would you?"

Mrs Bubble had a curious way of asking very obvious questions.

"No," said Jack, trying to squash his paper pellet beneath his hand. "No, I wouldn't."

"I rather thought not," said Mrs Bubble.

Mrs Bubble always knew the answer to her obvious questions. Jack didn't know why she asked them at all.

"Finish up to number ten in the book, please," said Mrs Bubble.

Jack sighed. Number ten seemed so far away, and he was not convinced of his need to know how many tomatoes he would be left with if he started with 57 and sold 29 of them at the market. He didn't like tomatoes, so he was hardly likely to grow them and sell them, was he? And if he did have 57, and sold 29, then he would give all the remaining ones to poor people or leave them in a ditch or something because he certainly didn't want to have any left. That would leave him with none at all. He wrote the answer in his book, along with his reasoning. It seemed to take up much more space than that allotted for a number, but he had learnt in the past that it was best to explain his answers. Mrs Bubble was sure to ask how he had reached a big fat '0'. It would save him explaining later.

The explanation covered the next two sums, which left only two more. They were about similarly irrelevant things so it didn't take long to finish. He was in the process of drawing illustrations along the margin of his book when the bell rang for lunch and Mrs Bubble began to say, "Alright, time to..."

Jack was up in a flash, part of the melee of boys and girls who were thrusting exercise books at Mrs Bubble, pushing pens and pencils into cases, and tripping over each other, desperate to escape, knowing that every precious second counted. Jack felt a slight misgiving as he thrust his own exercise book at Mrs Bubble and met her beady eyes.

"Thank you, Jack," she said.

Jack had an uncomfortable prickly feeling that he didn't

actually deserve Mrs Bubble's thanks. He knew that he hadn't tried his hardest and that his answers, reasoned though they were, were not really what she wanted.

He picked up his rucksack that had his lunch – his favourite marmite and cheese sandwiches – inside and headed out into the sunshine. It was hard, this nagging prickling in his mind. It kept reminding him that he was a Christian and that he ought always to be trying his best because that's what would please the Lord Jesus. And ever since Jack had trusted in the Lord Jesus who had died for him, and asked for all the wrong things he had done to be forgiven, he had these funny nagging feelings that he ought to be doing the right thing to please the Lord Jesus.

Jack had told Grandad about Mrs Bubble and how hard it was to be good at school. Grandad told Jack that he should think about doing everything he did for the Lord Jesus[1]. So you could be nice to someone, and it would be for the Lord Jesus; and you could be polite to Mrs Bubble, and it would be for the Lord Jesus; you could do what you were told, and it would be for the Lord Jesus; and you could work hard on your maths sums…

Jack was walking thoughtfully down the path to the school playing fields when he was interrupted by a shout from a big boy called Timmy Trial. Timmy was not Jack's friend. He was older than Jack and in a different class: in fact, the oldest class in the school. But no one at school ignored Timmy for long: partly because he was the biggest boy in the whole school, partly because he had the loudest voice, and partly because he was the school bully.

"Merrywhatsit!" shouted Timmy. "Come here!"

Jack, who could be surprisingly courageous even when he trembled inside, pretended he couldn't hear Timmy. He wanted to be invisible and go to the secret gap in the hedge to see if Grandad was combining close to the big sheds. He might take his friend Alfie with him, but he did *not* want Timmy.

"I said Merry-boy!" Timmy was never long ignored. And if Jack didn't want a black eye after school when the teachers couldn't see and no one dared to tell, he had better comply.

"What?" demanded Jack as boldly as he dared.

"I said come here!" hollered Timmy.

"I've got things to do," said Jack, and he began to walk faster in the direction of the outskirts of the school playing field, wondering at his own temerity. He knew that he could just about outrun Timmy Trial. Although Timmy was much bigger than he was, he was much bulkier too and Jack Merryweather was one of the fastest runners at school. Perhaps, if he managed to avoid Timmy today, Timmy might have forgotten Jack's behaviour by Monday. And Monday seemed a long time away.

Jack set off at a run. He heard the roar of Timmy Trial; vaguely heard the laughter of Timmy's so-called friends who were all scared of him; and he knew that no one would interfere to stop Timmy. He did not falter or slow his sprint for the gap in the hedge until he reached it and then, without even a backward glance, he plunged through.

It was like a different world on the other side of the hedge. Of course, Jack had not intended to leave the school grounds: that was strictly forbidden. But the need to escape from Timmy had precipitated this disobedience and he stood, suddenly alone, on the edge of Grandad's field of golden barley which waved and rippled gently in the warm breeze. The big farm sheds were close by and, without another thought, Jack set off at a jog to reach them and rounded the first massive structure with nothing but safety in his mind.

It was nearly silent here. There was no combine harvester

working in the field today; no reassuring presence of Grandad tinkering with something in the sheds; there was only the faint sound of children calling to each other as they enjoyed their lunch break in the school grounds, and the screechy call of a lone pheasant, hidden safely in the standing barley. The large sheds were closed and ominously silent.

Jack wondered whether he might hide with the pheasant in the field of barley, screened by the thick, standing grain. But the path he would make trampling down Grandad's crop would give him away. His only hope of hiding was somewhere in the big sheds which were stacked with all kinds of interesting farm implements and last season's leftover bales of straw. He was on familiar territory here, and, as the angry shout from Timmy got closer, he made for the big shed door and prayed frantically that it might somehow, magically, against all of Grandad's usual careful habits, be open.

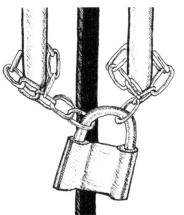

And then he saw the chain and padlock hanging from the door.

It was big and strong and most definitely *locked*.

20 The Rescue Of Timmy Trial

CHAPTER 2
BEHIND THE DOOR

"What do you think you're doing, Merry?" demanded Timmy Trial, as, panting and hot and flushed bright red, he stumbled around the corner of the farm shed and faced Jack.

Jack, trying to hide his dismay at the locked shed door, decided that a literal answer was his safest option. "I came to see my Grandad's sheds," he said. "I told you I had things to do."

Timmy stared at him. Timmy could talk a great deal about himself and how good he was at everything. He could talk a lot about how rich and important his Dad was. And he could beat up any kid in the school. But Jack had noticed before now that Timmy wasn't the best at dealing with cool, calm, logic. It was a convenient thing to remember.

"My Dad has got bigger sheds than these," said Timmy, looking around with a show of disdain.

Jack shrugged. Timmy always said things like that.

"You'll get into trouble for leaving school," said Timmy.

Jack shrugged again. "So will you," he replied.

Timmy was clearly startled as he realised, for the first time, this undeniable fact. It did not occur to him before now that they were both in the same predicament.

"I was following you!" said Timmy.

Jack kicked a small stone at his feet. He was glad that Timmy appeared to have forgotten that Jack was due at least one hard punch for ignoring him and running away. In fact, Timmy wasn't concentrating on Jack at all. He was looking at the second, smaller farm shed in some surprise.

"What's that?" he demanded.

Jack turned to look more closely at the shed that had drawn Timmy's attention. And then he looked again, moving closer, following Timmy, both boys drawn slowly and irresistibly to what should have been an ordinary farm shed. There was a strange sign above the door to the shed.

"What's Aletheia?" asked Timmy, peering at the sign.

Jack didn't like to admit that he had never heard of Aletheia. Since they were his Grandad's sheds Jack thought that he ought to know what Aletheia was and what it was doing there. "I think Grandad changed the shed," he said.

Timmy shot him an impatient glance. "I can see that," he

said. "What does it mean?"

"It's the entry to Aletheia," said Jack.

Timmy snorted. "Entry to Aletheia," he said, reading the sign. "Well, that's obvious isn't it, Merry? It says that there!" He pointed to the large sign which was hanging above the door of the smaller farm shed, which unambiguously stated, '*Entry to Aletheia*'. "Is your old Grandad making money from it?" asked Timmy. "I'll ask my Dad if he's ever heard of a business called *Aletheia*." He sounded derisive, as if Jack's Grandad was stupid and not half as good as Timmy's Dad.

"Well, if you really want to know," said Jack, annoyed at Timmy, "why don't you go and have a look?"

Timmy looked uncertain and Jack was pleased. Secretly he was every bit as unsure as Timmy was about approaching the shed: it had changed so dramatically that it didn't look like a farm shed at all. It not only had the strange sign about the unknown Aletheia above the door, but now it looked more like an odd sort-of office: with lots of windows, with people clearly moving about inside, with wide steps leading to the entrance door which didn't look anything like the entrance to a farm shed.

"Are you going in then?" asked Jack.

"Well, you go first then," returned Timmy, scowling at Jack, "otherwise I know it's a trick!"

Jack shrugged, as if it didn't matter to him one way or another; as if he were used to exploring the shed-office that was now called Aletheia. "Alright," he said.

And Jack led the way up the new entrance steps to the unknown door.

The entrance door clicked shut behind the two boys and their eyes gradually adjusted to the dimness of the office after the bright, hot sunshine they had left behind. At first it seemed that they were in a building not unlike a very ordinary office. Around them they could hear the murmur of voices, the faint hum of a machine, the tapping of keys as if someone was working at an old fashioned typewriter. It all sounded quietly business-like, as if the people working around them were meant to be there; everyone apart from them of course.

"Is Aletheia a business?" whispered Timmy. "Does it make lots of money?"

Jack was heartened by the fact that Timmy was whispering. He thought that now was as good a time as any to hint that he didn't have a clue what was going on.

"I don't really know," said Jack.

They were standing in the reception area of the office which was a bit like the one at school. There were sliding glass panels behind which were a large desk, a chair, and something that looked like a computer screen except that the writing on it looked like someone's handwriting. It said, 'Contamination Detector' in big letters which flashed on and off. There was no one in sight and on the glass panel there was a handwritten note which simply said, *'Dealing with Snares. Back soon.'*

Timmy stared at the note. "What on earth are…?"

"I don't know," said Jack, wishing Timmy would stop asking questions he didn't know the answer to.

There were pegs on the wall close to the glass screened area. The nearest one was labelled 'Mr Hardy Wallop, Supervisor', and there was a navy blue coat with lots of shining silver buttons neatly hung there. It looked like the posh uniform of a very important man. Timmy reached and touched one of the shiny buttons.

"What is this?" he asked.

"It's a coat of course," said Jack, glad he could answer at least one question.

"Well, I know *that*," retorted Timmy, his voice getting louder. "Of course I know *that*! I only meant that since we're in *your* Grandad's shed…" He made it sound like an accusation, as though Jack should know perfectly well what strange place they had come to.

"Well, *you* wanted to come," said Jack, sticking to the obvious and avoiding the unexplainable.

"Is it a secret?" asked Timmy, and his eyes gleamed. "I bet your Grandad isn't paying tax or is making something *illegal* here. Perhaps the Contamination Detector is about nuclear waste or something, right in our village!"

"Don't be stupid," said Jack, nettled at the accusation.

"Well, if it's not that, then what *is* this place?"

"If you really want to know, why don't you ask *him*?" said Jack, pointing at a closed door which was labelled in neat, gold lettering 'Mr Wallop, Supervisor of Entry to Aletheia'. He watched Timmy hesitate. "Go on, unless you're scared!" said Jack.

Timmy glanced back at the entrance door. And then he made a sudden move. "Alright!" he said, "watch this!" and he darted to Mr Wallop's door and knocked three times: loud, sharp raps on the door which shattered the quiet of the office. Then Timmy flung himself at the entrance door with a triumphant yell.

Jack hadn't known that Timmy was capable of moving so quickly but he might have guessed that Timmy's plan was to leave Jack to face the consequences with the disturbed Supervisor called 'Mr Wallop'. But, oddly enough, Timmy's attempted escape failed spectacularly. The entrance door stuck fast and remained immovable despite Timmy's efforts to yank it open, and the two boys faced each other across the reception area in sudden, disquieting silence. They both glanced at Mr Wallop's office door. And then back at each other again.

"It's stuck," hissed Timmy, pulling at the unyielding entrance door again. "Is it a trap? Why have you brought me here?"

"I didn't bring you," retorted Jack. "You followed me, remember?"

"What *is* this place?" demanded Timmy. "What *is* Aletheia? I know it's illegal!"

"You don't know anything," said Jack, feeling that was about the only thing he could be certain of at that moment.

Then both boys froze in sudden silence as the closed door to Mr Wallop's office slowly opened and a tall, stern, most forbidding man emerged.

"Aletheia is certainly not illegal anyway," said the tall man in a gruff, displeased tone. He had thick, dark eyebrows, a bushy moustache and a fierce look in his dark eyes. He wore a navy blue suit with bright silver buttons, just like the ones on the overcoat on the peg that Timmy had examined. He looked like a General in the army. He looked very important.

"*He* told me to knock," said Timmy, pointing at Jack.

Jack saw Timmy surreptitiously try the door handle again, as if he could escape from the office and leave Jack alone to face the consequences. But the door remained jammed shut.

"I see," said the tall man, Mr Wallop. "And do you always do what he says?"

"No!" spluttered Timmy, indignant at the very thought of following Jack Merryweather's lead in anything. "But...well, they're *his* Grandad's sheds!"

Jack could see that this did not make sense to the tall, stern Supervisor man. "I see," the man said, "that's how you came here, is it?"

Timmy hesitated, puzzled at the question. "Of course it is," he said, sounding, however, more polite than usual.

"We were at Grandad's sheds," added Jack.

The Supervisor, Mr Wallop, considered this. "I see," he said at last. "There are many ways to get to Aletheia from other countries and towns. I've never heard of Grandad's Sheds, but that's interesting, very interesting."

Jack wasn't sure how to explain that his own country wasn't called Grandad's Sheds. It was a surprise to him that this formidable man, who appeared to be in his right mind, was talking to them as if they had entered another place altogether: a place called Aletheia.

Timmy was looking at Mr Wallop as if he was certain the man was completely barmy. But he was clearly too much in awe of him to make such an accusation. "I think we should go now," Timmy said as firmly as he could. "We're going to be in trouble at school."

Jack didn't bother to say that Timmy had never before shown any concern for being in trouble at school. Timmy was always in trouble at school.

Mr Wallop did not appear concerned about them being in trouble at school either. "You'll be back at school in plenty of time," he said, as if he was quite certain of this. "Now, where's Tilly?" Mr Wallop looked at the vacant reception desk.

"It says she's dealing with Snares," said Jack, wondering whatever it meant.

"Ah," the Supervisor took a step closer, read the note, and nodded without surprise. "That explains it," he said. "We've had a run of contamination from Meddlers and Snares, and last week we even had a Sloth at work! We hardly got any work done that day! Well, I'll take you to get Checked In, although I really don't know why you couldn't find the way!" He still sounded stern, and Jack realised that there was a big sign on the wall behind reception which said, 'Checks Room this way,' with an arrow pointing further down the hallway.

Timmy was clearly incredulous, as if he was certain the whole conversation was gobbledygook. "Checked In?" he managed to splutter. "Checked In *where…?*"

The Supervisor interrupted Timmy sternly. "*Where?*" he repeated, as if he feared Timmy might be stupid or even mad. "Why, into Aletheia of course!"

CHAPTER 3
THE ADVENTURE BEGINS

The Supervisor, Mr Wallop, led the two boys to another room which was further down the hallway from the reception area. The door of this room was labelled in the same neat, gold lettering as the Supervisor's door. It simply stated, 'Checks Room'. Mr Wallop ushered them into the Checks Room and then left them there, clearly still wondering why they had not managed to find their way to the room unassisted, instead of disturbing him in his private office.

"This is mad!" Timmy hissed in Jack's ear as they stood in a room which, although undoubtedly nothing like a farm shed, was far more normal than they might have expected. Jack ignored Timmy. He wished that his friend Alfie was with him and not Timmy who was proving so tiresome.

Jack looked around the room. It was a large room full of interesting things. It was comfortable too, as if someone had moved their lounge into the office so that people felt at home there. There were chairs and sofas and cushions and small tables making cosy clusters around the room; there were pictures and posters on the walls; there was a big fireplace, empty of a fire and filled with a pretty arrangement of colourful flowers; and there were shelves of books of all types and colours and sizes. Several people were in the room, sitting in the chairs and browsing through the books. At the far end of the room there were more people who stood waiting at polished counters. They were facing members of staff in smart, navy blue uniforms with silver buttons, a bit like the Supervisor wore.

"Who are they?" demanded Timmy, looking at the people in uniform. "Are they Police? What do they want with *us* anyway?"

"I expect they'll lock you up," said Jack.

"They might be kidnappers or anything!" said Timmy.

"I don't think anyone would want to kidnap *you*," said Jack.

Timmy was uncertain whether this was intended as an insult or a compliment. "I'll pay you back for this, Merry," he said, settling for his usual threats and bluster. "You wait until we're back at school…!"

"Perhaps we'll never go back," said Jack.

"Not go back!" exclaimed Timmy. "You wait! My Dad will find me! You wait until my Dad finds out what your Grandad has been doing at his sheds…!"

Jack ignored him again. He was most interested in a strange, startling object in the centre of the room and he went towards it with Timmy following closely. It was a very big, oval shaped glass which appeared to contain crystal clear water. It was surely a huge water machine, and the water, when Jack looked at it, looked wonderfully, most unusually enticing, with sparkles of dark and light and all the colours of the rainbow swirling and shining like diamonds, as if the water was a living spring. Etched on the huge dome were the words '*Water of Sound Doctrine*'.

"What is it?" asked Timmy, pressing his nose up against the glass with a look of disgust.

Jack sighed. Talk about asking stupid questions all the time! "It's water of course," he said. "It says, 'Water of Sound Doctrine'."

Timmy punched his arm. "I'm not stupid!" he said. "But that's not clean water! No one could drink *that*!"

Jack rubbed his arm ruefully and wondered if Timmy was affected by some sort of madness, sunstroke perhaps. Didn't people see funny things in water when they had sunstroke…?

"Look," Jack took a cup from the neatly stacked pile by the huge water machine. "I'll drink some and show you."

"You're going to drink *that?*" Timmy asked incredulously.

Jack put his cup to the shiny tap at the bottom of the water dome. Crystal clear water gushed out and quickly filled the cup to the top. Then, to the sound of Timmy's wild protestations, Jack took an eager sip.

It was simply the best water in the world. It was just sweet enough but not too much so, with a subtle hint of all the nicest flavours he could possibly imagine. Fruity, and tangy, and sweet, and smooth, and ice cold, yet not so that it hurt your teeth and your head; everything about it was absolutely right, and exactly suitable, and for the first time on that hot day, Jack felt truly refreshed.

"Mad!" exclaimed Timmy. "Completely barmy! What if they blame me when you're poisoned and die and never come back from Aletheia, or wherever we are?"

"Then I expect you'll go to prison," said Jack. "Or at least you'll be sent miles away from home to some work camp to reform you."

Timmy flushed an angry red, but whether he was actually going to lunge at Jack in the middle of the Checks Room, in front of the polished counters and uniformed people that lined the far wall, Jack never did find out: because at that moment, across the room, a clear voice suddenly called, "Timothy Eustace Trial, please."

"I didn't know your middle name was Useless," said Jack.

Timmy didn't seem to hear Jack's comment about his middle name. His face was a picture of panic and defiance as he glanced wildly at the uniformed man who had called his name.

"What do they want?" asked Timmy. "What do they want with *me*? How do they even know my name?"

"They're probably just going to talk to you," said Jack.

He was surprised at how scared Timmy was, and although he didn't have a clue what he and Timmy were being 'Checked In' for, oddly he did not feel afraid. The water was somehow comforting and he began to notice, as he glanced at the pictures on the walls and the books on the shelves, that everything seemed to be to do with the Bible. Jack drew closer. He picked up a book in the section of the shelves under the letter 'S'. It was entitled 'Beware of Snares' and on the front there was a scary picture, of a shadowy creature with cold, glittering eyes.

He thought of the note pinned to the glass in reception about 'dealing with Snares'. He looked closely at the picture. Could it really be that there were real, live scary creatures in Aletheia that weren't in England and the rest of the world? He wished he'd paid more attention when they did a project about Africa at school. He had written an adventure about being chased by lions and tigers, but had Mrs Bubble told them anything about *Snares*?

"Jack Arnold Merryweather!" Jack suddenly heard his own name called by a young man at the counters. He was sorry that they knew about the 'Arnold' bit of his name; he wasn't particularly keen on it himself and he hoped that Timmy hadn't heard.

"I'm Jack," he said when he stood before the shiny wooden counter, looking at the young man peering at him through round, serious-looking glasses. He read his name badge: '*Herbert Wallop, Trainee Checker*'. Perhaps he was related to Mr Wallop, the Supervisor, but he didn't look as scary as the Supervisor. He was tall and skinny and there was a reassuring twinkle in his eyes.

"Well, of course you're Jack!" said Herbert Wallop. "Could I have your Identification first, please?"

"Oh," said Jack. "I don't think I have any...any of that on me..."

"How about in your pockets?" suggested Herbert.

Jack searched his pockets and found his spy watch, a five pence piece, a red piece of lego, leftover bits of biscuit, and a folded piece of paper. Herbert considered the piece of lego with great interest, turning it over in his hand and examining it closely. Reluctantly he returned it to Jack.

"I'll take the paper I think," said Herbert. He was very cheerful and seemed to be quite certain about the paper, so Jack handed it to him.

"*Dear Supervisor of Aletheia,*" Herbert read aloud from the paper which had come from Jack's pocket. "*I think you would like to meet Jack Merryweather, who might enjoy a visit to Aletheia and could learn more about Christian life there.*"

"Oh," said Jack. "Who is it from?"

"From your Grandad," said Herbert. "Well, that's all in order." He glanced down at the form he was completing that had *Jack Arnold Merryweather* written at the top of it. He scribbled something on the form and then he put a big tick by the first box, 'Identification'.

"The next section we have to complete is about what you thought of the Water of Sound Doctrine," said Herbert. He smiled encouragingly at Jack.

Jack glanced around at the huge dome of water which stood in the middle of the room. Now that he considered it again it seemed even bigger than the first time he had seen it. He wondered if it had changed size. "Umm…" Jack wondered what was expected of him. "Well, I did drink some of the water," he offered.

"And…" prompted Herbert.

Jack was bemused.

"Well, what did you see in the water?" prompted Herbert again.

Jack thought about the wonderful crystal clear water. "Just me," he said. "I saw my reflection."

"It was dirty!" Timmy's strident voice sounded loudly across the murmuring of various conversations in the room and Jack realised that they had only reached section two on Timmy's form too. "It was dark and there were wriggling creatures in it! I think they were worms!"

Herbert caught Jack's look of astonishment.

"It was lovely water," said Jack. "There were colours and sparkles and everything!"

Herbert nodded. "Yes," he agreed, and he looked pleased as he wrote something firmly on section two of Jack's form.

"I think Timmy was just saying it was dirty…" Jack struggled to explain the boy that they probably thought was his friend. Somehow he felt responsible for Timmy being there and being rude about their lovely water.

Herbert completed what he was writing and then he looked up. "I think Timmy was telling the truth," he said.

Jack stared at him in disbelief.

"You see, the water is a reflection of what you are," said Herbert. "It represents the whole, balanced truth of the Bible, and if you're not a Christian, then you don't see anything good in it at all."

"I don't think Timmy is a Christian," said Jack.

"No," agreed Herbert. "But at least you brought him here. We must see how we can help him to understand how to become a Christian!"

Jack went a bit red. "Umm…I didn't exactly bring him here," he said, feeling ashamed, "he just…well, he followed me…" He didn't think he could adequately explain how Timmy had been chasing him and they had both ended up…well, wherever they were.

"Of course, not all Christians see clean water either," Herbert continued to explain. "If you're doing wrong things as a Christian and not living as a Christian should, then the water might appear dirty to you too."

Jack turned to look at the water again, pleased when it remained clear and sparkling. He didn't ever want to see clouds and dirt in that water.

"My father is *Sir* Rufus Trial!" Timmy was saying loudly in the background. "He's a very important man! And he's a Christian too!"

Jack wondered if anyone in this strange office would care about the importance of Sir Rufus Trial when they seemed to be dealing with quite different things, like Snares.

"Now we scan your heart," said Herbert, returning to the form he was completing about Jack. "That shows us for sure whether you're a Christian or not. Of course, I already know that you're a Christian but we'll do all the Checks anyway. You didn't bring a Bible with you by any chance, did you?"

"Umm, no, I didn't," said Jack.

"No problem," said Herbert, "no problem at all!"

Jack was intrigued when Herbert passed a book-shaped object – which looked like a Bible – across his heart and smiled when he looked at the indicator.

"Of course I knew the indicator light would be white," he said as he leaned over the form with Jack's name on it and wrote something else. "The water told me that!"

"I think it's time to go now!" Timmy's loud voice carried clearly across the room. "Jack, it's time to go!"

Herbert glanced at his watch. "We shut soon anyway," he said. "We finish early on Fridays. There's plenty of accommodation in Aletheia but I expect you and…your friend will come home with us."

"Umm…" Jack was uncertain how to explain that he and Timmy needed to return to school.

"Are you coming, Jack?" Timmy reached him and tugged his arm. "They can't keep us here, you know. That's kidnapping!"

But his voice died away when the tall figure of Mr Wallop the Supervisor appeared behind the polished counters.

Mr Wallop was examining the work of his staff and he glanced at the form he held in his hand. Then he looked closely at Timmy. He seemed to be reading Timmy's Aletheia Entry Form.

"You can't stop us!" said Timmy, beginning to edge towards the door.

"Stop you?" said Mr Wallop with mild surprise. "Why would I try to stop you?"

"I'm going!" said Timmy. "You're all bats here anyway!" And he headed as fast as he could to the entrance door.

Jack followed more slowly, wondering if the door would actually open this time.

Others from the office followed too.

Timmy reached the entrance door and flung it open with a triumphant cry.

But the farm sheds were gone; there was a strange road ahead; an unknown city loomed large close by; and Timmy tumbled down the steps into a world he did not know.

CHAPTER 4
INTO THE UNKNOWN

It took some time to calm Timmy Trial sufficiently so that an explanation could be heard above his panicked jabbering. Even then the explanation that Mr Wallop offered him did not calm his fears.

"A land called Err!" repeated Timmy. "I've never heard of a land called Err!"

"Maybe they don't teach them much at their school, Dad," said Herbert in what was intended to be a subtle undertone.

"Our school is at the top of the Schools' League Table!" said Timmy. "It's why my Dad chose it for me! Tell them Jack!"

Jack was becoming practiced at turning a deaf ear to Timmy's pleas for support.

"Well, I've certainly never heard of a country called Grandad's Sheds," said Mr Wallop. "It's quite possible that they might not have heard of Err or Aletheia there either."

Timmy looked at Jack, unable to articulate how mad he thought they all were. Jack avoided his glance. Ever since he had glimpsed the strange place outside of the door through which they had entered Grandad's shed, he was still coming to terms with the fact that he really did seem to be in the middle of a real, live, completely unexplainable adventure.

"There's no such place as Err, or Aletheia, or anything else!" yelled Timmy.

"Now, now," said Mr Wallop firmly. "There are all sorts of different places. Your Grandad's Sheds country, for example, that we had never heard of before today, but that doesn't mean that we don't believe it exists…"

Mr Wallop looked puzzled and frustrated when his well intentioned remonstrations with Timmy produced completely the opposite effect.

"There is no such place!" shouted Timmy. "No Err! No Aletheia! No Grandad's Sheds country! Are you all completely mad? No Err! No Aletheia…!"

"It was quite hot today, Dad," interjected Herbert, looking with curiosity at the hysterical boy. "Perhaps he's got sunstroke, or maybe he's not quite right in the head…?"

"Could be," said Mr Wallop.

Timmy laughed hysterically. "*Me* not right in the head!" he choked. "They think *I'm* the one that's not right in the head! Tell them, Merry! Explain to them…!"

"I think we really have come to a different place," said Jack, trying to be logical and wishing Timmy was a million miles away back at school, wherever that now was. "Otherwise, where exactly are we?"

"We've been kidnapped, that's where!" exclaimed Timmy.

"Being kidnapped isn't exactly a place," said Jack. He wondered why he had never before noticed how stupid Timmy was.

"Well, I know *that*!" said Timmy. "This is all *your* fault, Merry!"

Following Timmy's awful surprise that the outside of the office no longer contained the fields of their familiar village and that they were somewhere else entirely, Mr Wallop and Herbert helped the frantic boy back inside and they all returned to the comfortable interior of the Checks Room. Timmy was laid on a large sofa and Mr Wallop dispatched a nice girl called Tilly to make Timmy a cup of tea. Tilly wore the smart, silver-buttoned uniform of the office and was the receptionist who had been absent 'dealing with Snares' when they arrived. Jack wondered what that involved, and how Tilly, who was a petite girl, had managed to get rid of the Snares, whatever they were.

"I think you should come home with us tonight," said Mr Wallop as Jack browsed amongst the books again and drank the soothing Water of Sound Doctrine. "We often have visitors to stay and I think that would be safest for you."

Safest? Jack wondered what Mr Wallop wanted to keep them safe from, but Mr Wallop didn't say.

Timmy sipped his tea and stared moodily at them all. "Kidnappers," he muttered. But his tea, and the delicious chocolate cake that Tilly had passed around, seemed to revive Timmy's spirits and he began to look around with more interest.

Jack realised how hungry he was and that he had never eaten the lunch from his school rucksack which was, strangely enough, still on his back. It didn't seem right to eat his sandwiches in front of them all and not share them, so he stuck to the chocolate cake which was just about the nicest thing he had ever tasted. He saw Timmy take a second slice of the cake and was glad that Timmy's mouth was too full for more protests. There was comparative quiet in the room. Mr Wallop finished checking the forms his staff had completed that day, Herbert Wallop tidied his counter, and the nice girl Tilly tidied the Checks Room and made kind remarks to Timmy and Jack.

"What's that book?" asked Timmy.

Jack had once more been drawn to the book about Snares on the bookshelves. "It's about creatures called Snares," said Jack.

"There are no such things," said Timmy, getting off the sofa to join Jack and peering at the picture on the book cover.

Tilly looked surprised and then serious. "You must beware of Snares," she said. "There are many different types and they are everywhere you allow them to be. Of course, you need to be a Christian to really fight them successfully…"

"I am a Christian," interrupted Timmy. "My parents give lots of money to the local church and I'm as good as anyone else."

"That doesn't make you a Christian," said Tilly.

Timmy was not inclined to argue with Tilly who was really very nice. "Well, I'm not worried about Snares, anyway," he said.

Jack put the book about Snares back on the shelf and felt the uncomfortable pricking feeling in his mind that he had never told many of his friends, and certainly not Timmy, how he was a real Christian because he had trusted in the Lord Jesus[2] to save him from the punishment he deserved for the wrong things he had done, things that the Bible called sin[3]. Perhaps Timmy didn't even know how to become a real Christian.

Mr Wallop at last finished his checks, Herbert picked up his briefcase, Tilly slipped a bag over her shoulder and the other staff departed, talking cheerfully and saying goodbye. Then Mr Wallop ushered them all out into the bright sunshine of Aletheia.

The Entry to Aletheia office, which had been Grandad's shed, stood at the edge of a wide, well paved street called Pride Way that sloped steeply downwards, right to the edge of a city which they now knew was the city of Aletheia. There were golden fields of barley close by which was the only thing that vaguely reminded them of the world they had left behind. They were clearly on the edge of the city streets, just where the buildings stopped and the land turned to neat, well kept farmland.

Above them the bulk of the city of Aletheia rose stately and grand: with huge stone buildings and turrets and towers and crooked rooftops. Rising above it all, clear against the sky, there was a plain, unadorned cross. They loitered at the roadside as Mr Wallop locked up the Entry to Aletheia with many chains and padlocks. Herbert explained to them that the locks were necessary, not because there was much crime in Aletheia, but because the Entry to Aletheia moved to other locations that might be far less safe.

"Who moves it?" asked Jack.

"Nobody," said Herbert.

"Someone must move it," said Timmy, "it can't move by itself!"

"Why not?" asked Herbert, sounding puzzled.

"Things don't just move on their own!" said Timmy. "That's impossible!"

Herbert looked warily at Timmy, as if he was afraid that further disagreement might precipitate another episode of hysterics. "Well, it does move," he said, "and tomorrow it will be somewhere else."

"Where?" asked Jack.

Herbert looked perplexed at his question. "Well, I don't know yet," he said, as if he feared they might be slow to understand the most elementary things. "It's not tomorrow yet, is it? We won't know where it's moved until it's moved."

"Completely barmy," Timmy muttered to Jack.

Herbert heard and he seemed to be amused. "Perhaps things are different at Grandad's Sheds than they are here," he said.

Timmy groaned and seemed to be on the point of protesting so Herbert quickly began to point out things that he thought might interest them from their vantage point on the hillside of the city of Aletheia.

They looked down Pride Way. It turned to wide marble steps towards the edge of the city, just before the boundary of sparkling water that appeared to encircle the entire town.

"There are four bridges over the water into Aletheia," explained Herbert, "and four main roads in and out of the city which go North, South, East and West."

"What is that water?" asked Jack, looking at the glinting water. "Is it like a moat?"

"It's the Water of Sound Doctrine," said Herbert.

"The same as the water in the Checks Room?" asked Jack.

"Yes," said Herbert. "It's the only safe drinking water in the land and certainly the only drinking water for a Christian!"

Jack glanced at Timmy who merely made a face. Timmy wasn't

interested in the water that he had found so disgusting; instead he was distracted. He was watching the vacant sky with avid attention and all at once he flung out his hand and snatched something from the air. He slowly opened his fingers and looked in astonishment at the small gold coin that lay there. It had the image of an eagle on it and clearly said 'The Land of Err' and 'One Erona'. But most surprisingly of all were the fragile, transparent, gold tinted wings that were even now fluttering feebly as if it was anxious to fly again. For a moment Timmy was speechless at the evidence before his own eyes. Jack also stared at the small coin whose strange wings were trying to unfurl themselves.

Herbert peered over their shoulders and merely shrugged. "It's unusual to catch one," he said, clearly startled at Timmy. It seemed that Herbert was not at all surprised that money could fly; he was only surprised that Timmy had been able to catch some.

"But it's money," said Timmy in an awestruck tone.

"Umm…yes, it is," said Herbert with a patient but perplexed expression on his good-natured face. Timmy's astonishment that money could fly did not reassure Herbert regarding Timmy's state of mind.

"It was flying!" said Timmy. "Money was flying!"

"Yes, of course" said Herbert. "That's what it does when we love it too much. It flies away."

"Wow," murmured Jack wonderingly.

"Doesn't it do that at…umm…in your country?" asked Herbert.

"No it doesn't!" said Timmy. "Tell him, Jack!"

"It's in the Bible," said Herbert. "Riches make themselves wings and fly away[4]."

Timmy clearly thought that Herbert was crazy: but he couldn't doubt the evidence in his own hand. And as he watched, the small coin unfurled its delicate, transparent, gold tinted wings, and suddenly it was gone.

"Oh well," said Herbert, "it was only one Erona. You couldn't have bought much with that!"

They did not see it go, so fast was its flight, and Timmy's expression was a curious mixture of incredulity and cunning as he searched the sky around them for the sight of glittering gold.

"You won't find any more," said Herbert. "Usually they fly too high to catch. Many people have wasted their lives trying to find ways of catching and keeping the riches now flying around in the sky. Not usually the people in Aletheia, of course, but out in Err.

The people in Love-of-Riches have spent a fortune trying to find a way of keeping it. But of course that just makes it fly faster!"

"How does anyone have any money at all then?" asked Jack, trying to understand the laws of this strange land where money could grow wings and fly away.

"If you don't love it too much then it doesn't fly away!" explained Herbert. He looked anxiously at Timmy who, curiously enough, no longer seemed to question or begrudge their strange adventure.

Instead Timmy was looking with anticipation towards the land of Err.

CHAPTER 5
THE CITY OF ALETHEIA

Mr Wallop finished securing the Entry to Aletheia office and they all began to walk up the hill towards the centre of the city of Aletheia where the Wallops had their home. Timmy was preoccupied and didn't say much. Jack saw Timmy constantly scanning the sky around him. Timmy was searching for an elusive glint of golden money flying through the air and he hardly seemed to see the sights of the city at all.

The wide road seemed to grow steeper with every step they took upwards, and massive, ornate stone buildings towered impressively above them. There was a huge fortress with stone columns and towers, at the top of which was a flag showing a

white cross. The fortress looked very strong and secure.

"That's the Academy of Soldiers-of-the-Cross," explained Mr Wallop. "My oldest son, Harold, is training to be a Rescuer there."

"A Rescuer of what?" asked Timmy, stopping his eager search of the sky and looking momentarily interested in the fortress.

"A Rescuer of those who are astray," said Mr Wallop.

"I expect they're like Police," Timmy said to Jack. "They probably give people directions when they get lost and stuff."

Mr Wallop didn't comment on Timmy's conclusion about Rescuers but Jack didn't think that Timmy could be right at all. Jack was watching the people that were coming and going to the Academy of Soldiers-of-the-Cross, and to his astonishment there were people among them *actually wearing armour*!

"I don't think they look like Police," said Jack. "They're more like soldiers, like warriors actually. Look at their armour!"

"Armour!" echoed Timmy. "What armour?"

"I expect they're going out into Err on missions, or else returning," explained Mr Wallop. "That's why they'll be wearing their armour."

"There is no armour!" said Timmy.

"But…" began Jack.

"He can't see it," said Herbert.

"Can't see it…!" spluttered Timmy.

"Only Christians can see another Christian wearing the armour of God[5]," explained Herbert. "Apart from our weapon the Bible of course, that's the exception. Anyone can see the Bible."

"Oh, of course," said Timmy sarcastically. "Anyone can see the Bible!"

"Real armour," said Jack in awe.

"For real enemies," said Mr Wallop soberly.

"And what kind of *weapon* is a Bible anyway?" scoffed Timmy.

"The Bible is the sword of the Spirit which is the Word of God[6]," said Mr Wallop. "But don't worry," he added to Timmy, "there's plenty that we can teach you during your time with us to help you understand what it means to become a Christian."

"I am…" began Timmy indignantly, but he was interrupted by Mr Wallop greeting two men who stood at the side of the road outside of the Academy.

"Captain Steadfast!" said Mr Wallop, and he shook hands with a tall man in armour who looked every inch a Captain.

"A Captain!" said Timmy, but he didn't sound so doubtful; even if Timmy could not see his armour, it was clear that he was impressed by the big man.

Captain Steadfast looked keenly at the two boys.

"Captain Ready Steadfast is the Deputy Chief Rescuer of Err," said Mr Wallop.

It all sounded most impressive and even Timmy did not mock the title which really meant nothing to him or Jack at all.

"This is Mr Wonky Dollar," said Captain Steadfast, and he drew forward the man next to him. Mr Dollar appeared very odd beside the tall, smart Captain. He was a shabby man, he stooped towards the ground, and he shuffled his feet as if he was unhappy to be there and anxious to get away.

"We've been trying to persuade Mr Dollar to stay a while longer in Aletheia," said Captain Steadfast.

"I've been here quite long enough," said Wonky Dollar. "I was told it would benefit me but there are no opportunities for me here, and it seems money flies away as easily here as anywhere else! I lost one Erona earlier when I was carrying out an experiment with my new treasure boxes!" and when he put his hands into his pockets there were strange jangling and clanking noises there.

Captain Steadfast shook his head. "It isn't money that can benefit you here, Wonky," he said, but Mr Dollar interrupted.

"I've heard all I want to about what Aletheia can do for me," he said, "and now I must be on my way to try my fortunes elsewhere!"

"It isn't Aletheia that can help you as such," said Mr Wallop, "although Aletheia is the place that stands for the Truth. But it's the message of the cross that is the answer. Because of what the Lord Jesus has done there, anyone who trusts in Him…"

But Mr Dollar didn't want to know, and when he could, he drew closer to the two boys and away from the others as Mr Wallop and Herbert and Captain Steadfast talked together.

"Did you say you lost a small coin earlier?" asked Timmy, eyeing Mr Dollar with interest.

Mr Dollar nodded. "I was experimenting with ways of slowing down the flight of riches," he said. "I'm sure it can be done, and one day I'll be the one who finds out how to clip their wings!"

"I found your coin!" exclaimed Timmy. He looked at Mr Dollar as if he was sensing a sudden opportunity. He wasn't impressed with Wonky Dollar's appearance, but he was more than interested in his lost riches.

"Did you catch it again?" asked Mr Dollar. "It was only a one Erona piece but if you caught it then it means I might have slowed its flight after all!"

"Yes," said Timmy, "I caught it but then it flew away again."

"A pity," said Mr Dollar, "but still, that's an improvement. It means that they *can* be caught!"

Jack looked at Mr Dollar with his scruffy clothes and frayed, patched jacket (which wasn't even as good as the jacket that Grandad wore for feeding the cows!). Whatever Mr Dollar was inventing to catch and keep his riches, it hadn't worked yet. Did all his riches just keep flying away?

"Do you have anything you'd like to invest?" Mr Dollar asked the two boys with a hasty, concerned glance at Captain Steadfast whom he evidently didn't want to overhear him. "What do you have in your pockets?"

Timmy hesitated. He was very careful with his money even though he generally had a lot of it, but he was reluctant to share it with this scruffy stranger. "I might have some ideas for helping you catch money," he said cautiously.

Mr Dollar did not immediately attend to Timmy. He was

looking eagerly at the contents of Jack's pockets as Jack removed his spy watch, a five pence piece, and a red piece of lego. The piece of paper was gone. Herbert had kept that for Jack's 'Aletheia File'. And the biscuit crumbs must have disappeared the last time he emptied his pockets.

Mr Dollar looked with some mistrust at the watch and the small five pence piece. Then he picked up the piece of lego and his eyes gleamed. "Curious," he said examining it closely, "very curious! I wonder... Do you mind if I borrow this, young man?"

"It's not exactly money," said Jack. "I don't think it will make you rich."

"It's a piece of lego!" said Timmy. "It's nothing at all!"

But Mr Dollar shook his head in a most determined way. "If you'll lend this to me," he said, "I'll turn it into gold!"

Jack was extremely doubtful but he felt very sorry for Mr Dollar. "You can have it if you want," he said, and watched Mr Dollar hastily secure the piece of lego with locks and chains in one of his many clanking treasure boxes.

Timmy was looking at Mr Dollar in disbelief. "Is there a way of turning...umm, completely normal things into gold?" he asked in a hushed tone. He drew closer to Mr Dollar, trying to avoid the others overhearing his whispered discussion with him.

Jack was alarmed. He was glad that Timmy had calmed down and was inclined to be reasonable about their adventure, but he didn't think things were going in the right direction with Timmy taking up with someone like Mr Wonky Dollar. He tried to hear what they were saying, tried to catch Mr Wallop's or Herbert's eye where they stood talking with Captain Steadfast. Whatever the murmured exchange between Timmy and Wonky Dollar involved it did not seem likely that it would lead to Timmy being helped to see his own need of being saved and becoming a Christian.

Uneasily Jack watched as Mr Dollar at last hastened away, slipping through the lengthening shadows, taking the easy slope downwards and out of the city of Aletheia, into the land of Err.

They made one further stop on their journey through the city to the Wallops' home. Mr Wallop announced that he thought they had time to stop and see someone he referred to as 'Grandpa Able'. They left the crowded buildings of the city behind them and crossed neat, lush parkland to the large Rest Home which was part of the Run-the-Race Retirement Complex. Herbert explained that Grandpa Able was Mr Wallop's Grandpa, which Jack thought might make him hundreds of years old. But when they saw him, in a large lounge where lots of older people sat in big, comfy armchairs, Grandpa Able appeared to be surprisingly hearty and robust. He was sat with another man, and the two old men appeared to be carving small sticks.

"That's Mr Reuben Duffle," said Herbert. "He's Grandpa Able's best friend."

"He looks dead," Timmy said bluntly.

Mr Wallop frowned warningly at Timmy, but there was some truth in Timmy's assessment of old Mr Duffle. He was a tiny, wizened, faded old man who appeared to be held together only by the thick belt that bunched his trousers together at his waist. Otherwise it seemed he might blow away on the next fresh breeze and disintegrate entirely.

"Mr Duffle is a great man," said Mr Wallop as they drew closer to the two old men.

Mr Duffle did not look great at all but Mr Wallop greeted him with the utmost respect.

"I think he means an *old* man not a *great* man!" Timmy whispered to Jack.

Mr Wallop introduced the two boys.

"He looks barmy!" whispered Timmy.

"Barmy?" quavered Mr Duffle. "They call the boy Barmy, do they? Well I never!"

"Bats!" Timmy whispered indignantly to Jack.

"Barmy Bats, is it?" said Mr Duffle. "Strange sort of name, but then they come from a strange place, don't they?"

Timmy was speechless with indignation and Jack squashed the sudden urge to laugh and moved further away from Timmy and stood out of earshot of Timmy's whispers.

"Have you ever been to a place called Grandad's Sheds, Mr Duffle?" asked Mr Wallop.

"I went to Grandad's Sheds once for a holiday," said Mr Duffle in his feeble, quavering voice. He peered closely at Jack as if he might actually know him.

"Did you?" Jack stared back at him.

"Many years ago," said the old man. "Many, many years…"

He trailed off, his faded eyes seeing things that none of the others could see. Jack didn't know what to think. He was almost positive that Mr Duffle had not been to Grandad's sheds on holiday. But in Aletheia, well, he supposed that anything might happen. And besides, hadn't it been Grandad that had written that letter about Jack going to Aletheia? Perhaps Grandad knew old Mr Duffle…

Jack looked at Mr Duffle curiously. In one hand he was clutching a handful of small sticks and twigs on which he had made carvings. He solemnly handed one to Jack without seeming to know what he was doing.

Timmy sniggered and then protested as Mr Wallop's large hand settled tightly on his shoulder, and Timmy received his own gift of a small carved stick in sullen silence.

Jack put his carved stick in his pocket.

"Silly old duffer!" muttered Timmy as he freed himself from Mr Wallop's restraining hand and they departed. He threw the small stick he had received from Mr Duffle onto the grass at the side of the road. "Barmy!" he said.

"Barmy Bats," said Herbert cheerfully. "You know, I think that name suits you, Timmy!"

Herbert was taller than Timmy and Timmy ignored him. Jack stooped and picked up the twig that Timmy had thrown away. He put it in his other pocket. He wasn't sure why he picked it up, except that Mr Duffle seemed to think that it was of value and somehow it didn't seem right to throw it away.

"Mr Duffle was the Chief Rescuer in Err many years ago," said Mr Wallop. "He faced dangers and fought terrible things and helped people back to the cross in Aletheia from the most awful places. And now Mr Duffle is a man of prayer. He's still a warrior in his own way."

"We say prayers in church," said Timmy.

"The effective, fervent prayer of a righteous man avails much[7]," Mr Wallop quoted from the Bible.

And Jack knew that Mr Wallop meant that that was how Mr Duffle prayed.

Mr Wallop hurried them homewards as shadows began to lengthen in Aletheia and the hot afternoon sun began to lower in the sky. He was consulting his watch as they rounded the final corner and confronted the large, square, apartment block called 'Foundation-of-Faith Apartments.'

"Here we are! Home at last!" said Herbert, while Mr Wallop put his watch back into his pocket and murmured:

"Now I'm for it. We're late for dinner!"

CHAPTER 6
AT HOME WITH THE WALLOPS

The Wallops' apartment was the entire top floor of the Foundation-of-Faith Apartment block. Mr Wallop led them up the many flights of stairs to the top while Timmy protested about the lack of an elevator or lift of some sort to carry them there. It was not clear whether Mr Wallop or Herbert knew what he meant. What was clear was that Mr Wallop considered the state of Timmy's mind to be still fragile if not entirely unhinged, and he was anxious not to cause another scene with Timmy.

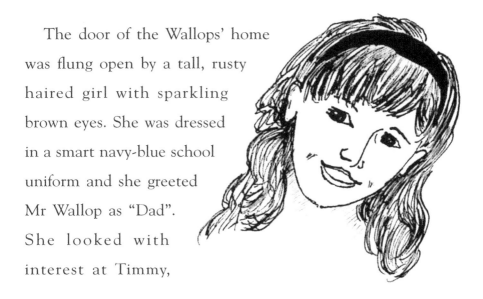

The door of the Wallops' home was flung open by a tall, rusty haired girl with sparkling brown eyes. She was dressed in a smart navy-blue school uniform and she greeted Mr Wallop as "Dad". She looked with interest at Timmy, who was very red in the face and out of breath from the number of stairs they had climbed.

"Well!" she exclaimed. "You're not very used to climbing stairs, are you, Fatso?"

"Henrietta," said Mr Wallop, "I do wish you would show some consideration for our guests. I don't suppose they're used to being greeted in this fashion." He glanced at Timmy who might have protested at being called 'Fatso'. But oddly enough Timmy was staring at Henrietta Wallop with an expression on his face that Jack had never seen before. It was the first time that Jack had ever seen Timmy lost for words.

"They're only boys," said Henrietta. "I'm sure Fatso doesn't mind being teased, do you, Fatso?" she added in a perfectly friendly tone to the still speechless Timmy. "And the other one…"

"I'm Jack Merryweather," said Jack.

"That's a good name," said Henrietta.

"Actually, my name is…" began Timmy.

"Where's your mother, Henry?" her father asked.

"Serving up dinner and commenting on how late you are," said Henrietta.

"I'm quite capable of speaking for myself thank you, Henrietta," said Mrs Wallop, coming into the hallway and wiping her hands down her apron. "Dinner's ready, Hardy, although it may well be burnt by now!" she said, but she was smiling and not really cross. She turned her attention to the two boys. "And who are our visitors…?"

"Fatso and Jack," said Henrietta, hanging up her father's coat and turning around to grin at the two boys.

"Actually my name is…" Timmy began with more determination.

"This is Hugo, my twin brother," said Henrietta, giving Timmy no chance to explain, and she pulled forward a tall boy with auburn hair who was very like her except that he had far less to say. "And this is Hezekiah, also known as Zek… Come Zek, they won't eat you…" and she presented the youngest of the family, a freckle faced boy who was a little younger and smaller than Jack.

"Jack and…" Mr Wallop endeavoured to make some sort of proper explanation about the boys but this time Herbert Wallop reappeared to interrupt; his jacket with silver buttons had vanished and in its place he was wearing a comfy, brown knitted jumper with holes in it.

"That's Barmy Bats!" said Herbert with a good natured grin.

"I am not…!" began Timmy, furious with Herbert and casting a strangely concerned glance at Henrietta Wallop.

"That's what Mr Duffle thought his name was!" said Herbert.

"Mr Duffle is usually right," commented Hugo.

"It's entirely your own fault that Mr Duffle came to imagine that your name is Barmy Bats, Timmy," said Mr Wallop.

"Barmy Bats is a catchy name," said Henrietta. "Imagine really being called something as interesting as Barmy Bats!"

Timmy was staring at Henrietta as if he were in the middle of some great conflict; as if he suddenly wasn't certain whether he should continue to protest at the ridiculous name of Barmy Bats…or actually embrace it.

"Anyway," said Henrietta, not at all uncertain about the matter, "whatever your name is, I'm going to call you Barmy Bats!"

Mrs Wallop was a very good cook. They all sat down to a wonderful dinner of roast beef (which wasn't burnt after all), with plenty of vegetables and gravy and Yorkshire puddings. There was loads for everybody despite the addition of two guests, and

Jack, who was very hungry and felt as if he'd been travelling in a strange country for a very long time, ate everything put in front of him and had second helpings besides. Timmy consumed even more than Jack. He had completely forgotten his earlier concerns at their strange adventure. It was just as if the two boys had expected to go to the Wallops for tea that Friday.

"Where are you from?" Mrs Wallop asked the two boys as they ate.

"They're from Grandad's Sheds," said Mr Wallop, sounding, however, uncertain of this fact and remembering the effect the mention of Grandad's Sheds seemed to have on Timmy. He didn't want another scene; just now he wanted peace to enjoy his second helping of mashed potatoes.

"Grandad's Sheds?" said Mrs Wallop. She sounded puzzled. "I don't think I've ever been there. I did quite a lot of travelling before I was married," she explained. "Is it far away?"

"Not exactly," said Jack. "You see, we really just came through the door in the shed. And then we were in the Entry to Aletheia."

"I see," said Mrs Wallop.

Timmy tried to explain, through a mouthful of roast beef and Yorkshire pudding, that there was no such place. "Tell them

Jack!" he managed to say at the end of his garbled explanation.

"Swallow your mouthful, Barmy," said Henrietta, and then giggled at the look on Timmy's face.

Jack was getting a little tired of this fairly constant plea of 'tell them Jack!' "I just told them," he said. It didn't really matter to him if these nice people thought that they came from a country called Grandad's Sheds. For all he knew they hadn't heard of England or Great Britain or anywhere normal anyway.

"It was very succinctly explained, thank you, Jack," said Mrs Wallop.

"They'll think we're mad!" muttered Timmy. "Grandad's Sheds indeed!"

"We might think you're mad anyway," said Henrietta.

"More eating, less talking, Henry," said her father.

"Barmy's taken the last Yorkshire pudding!" exclaimed Hezekiah.

"My name is *not* Barmy!" Timmy flared up. He glared at Hezekiah who looked surprised and went a bit red.

"If you can really manage another Yorkshire pudding, Barmy… umm, I mean Timmy…" said Mrs Wallop, "you can go ahead and eat it… Henrietta, will you please stop giggling!"

"What do you learn at your school in…well, wherever it is?" Hugo wanted to know.

Timmy swallowed his mouthful. "All sorts of things," he said. "Our school is at the top of the League Table! Tell them Jack!"

"I don't think they know what the League Table is," said Jack, catching Hugo's bemused expression and wondering if he would ever have room for the yummy apple crumble Mrs Wallop was beginning to serve.

"It means we're a superior school!" said Timmy.

"It's probably a different school for problem kids," Herbert said in an aside to his father, remembering the lack of knowledge that Timmy and Jack had earlier displayed about Aletheia and the land of Err.

"It is not!" retorted Timmy, overhearing him. "We're not stupid, you know!"

"Keep your hair on, Barmy!" said Henrietta. "Who cares what sort of school it is anyway?"

Timmy was clearly at a loss how to answer this. "Well, anyway," he said at last, "we do learn more useful things apart from things about the Bible. In fact, we don't really learn much about the Bible at all!"

Timmy's comment was met with stunned silence.

"Do you mean that you're not a Christian?" asked Hezekiah in a horrified tone. He had recently become a Christian himself and was very keen about it. He could not now imagine how anybody would not want to become a Christian and be safe from punishment for all the wrong things they had done, things the Bible called sin.

"Of course we're Christians!" said Timmy.

"I think Timmy means that some people in their country think that going to church and doing good and such means that you're a Christian," said Mr Wallop.

"Like the people in the town of Do-Good in Err," said Hugo.

"But that's not how to become a Christian at all!" said Henrietta. "Everyone in Aletheia knows that!"

"No, we all know that, of course," said Mr Wallop. "But there are plenty of people in Err and other countries that think as Timmy does, and we'll be trying to help Timmy while he's here…"

"I don't need help!" said Timmy. "I mean," he added quickly, catching Henrietta's sudden fierce glare, "that we just think differently, that's all! Tell them Jack!"

"I am a Christian," Jack said slowly. "I trusted in the Lord Jesus to take away my sins and that's when I became a Christian." And as soon as he'd said it he felt a tremendous relief. At last he had told someone, and it was Timmy Trial no less, that he was a real Christian.

"That's right!" said Hezekiah, "that's right, Jack! That's how you become a Christian…"

Hezekiah was the last to finish his crumble and ice-cream and had taken far too much. But he was determined to finish and was doggedly shoving spoonfuls into his mouth.

"You'll explode, Zek," Henrietta warned him.

"I won't explode," said Hezekiah, and belched unintentionally and very loudly.

"Hezekiah!" exclaimed Mrs Wallop.

Henrietta got a fit of giggles.

"We met Wonky Dollar with Captain Steadfast on our way home today," said Herbert.

"Ready Steadfast is so cool," said Hezekiah. He was hiccupping now which was adding to Henrietta's amusement.

"I gave Mr Dollar a piece of lego," said Jack, only now remembering this fact.

"He doesn't even know what it is, you duffer!" said Timmy, with a glance for approval at Henrietta.

"Duffer yourself!" retorted Henrietta.

"That was very kind of you, Jack," said Mrs Wallop, sounding vaguely puzzled.

"What is lego?" asked Hezekiah.

"Don't you know what lego is?" exclaimed Timmy.

"I'm sure it's something very nice," murmured Mrs Wallop, starting to stack the plates.

Jack wasn't sure how to explain what lego was. "You build things with it," he said.

"All the kids in our country have lego," said Timmy.

"Ooooh, hoity-toity!" mocked Henrietta. "Who wants lego anyway?"

"Henrietta," said her father wearily. Mr Wallop had at last picked up his evening newspaper called 'The Truth' and was entering his favourite, most peaceful part of the evening.

"What does Wonky Dollar want to build with lego?" asked Hugo.

"Money, I think," said Jack.

"You don't build money with lego!" scoffed Timmy, eager to impress. "But my father is…"

"Your father is probably King Barmy Bats!" retorted Henrietta.

Hezekiah hiccupped very loudly as he giggled at Henrietta's comment. Timmy's eyes narrowed on Hezekiah. Henrietta might say what she liked, and Hugo was taller than Timmy. But small Hezekiah Wallop was a very different matter. Jack recognised the look that Timmy gave Hezekiah. And he knew that the surroundings of Aletheia had not changed Timmy.

He knew that Timmy the bully was back.

CHAPTER 7
A SOUND IN THE NIGHT

After dinner Harold Wallop appeared. He was the oldest of Mr and Mrs Wallop's children and was training to be a Rescuer. He was big and tall and looked just like Jack imagined a Rescuer would: very tough and utterly dependable. Jack liked him at once. Harold had heard about the arrival of Jack and Timmy from Captain Steadfast and suggested that they might like to see something of Aletheia before it grew dark. Hugo and Henrietta and Hezekiah were loud in their approval of the idea and they accompanied Harold and the two boys out into the intriguing streets of the city just as the sun was finally sinking to rest for the night and the long summer twilight was settling quietly across Aletheia.

The centre of Aletheia was an interesting jumble of crowded old buildings of all types and sizes. They encroached onto cobbled streets, creating shadows and fascinating nooks and crannies and secret places. The children went first to Redemption Square which was where all the roads in Aletheia led. The square marked the highest, most central spot of the old city. It was quiet and tranquil as they entered it and Timmy's comments about the interesting streets they spied and his wish to explore them were silenced as they entered the square, and all the chatter died away. In the centre of the large square, accessible on every side, was the cross. It was set high at the top of many steps, clear and unmistakable, and unavoidable too.

Small streams sparkled and bubbled and threaded their way through Redemption Square and Harold explained that the streams were the source of the Water of Sound Doctrine. They ran mostly underground from the cross right to the boundary of Aletheia where they all flowed into the Water of Sound Doctrine that ran continuously around the city. Jack wondered whether Timmy saw the small streams by the cross as dirty too; but Timmy did not say.

"The cross is the beginning and the end to all the questions and answers about Christian life," said Harold Wallop when they all stood in the centre of the square.

"I don't see how," remarked Timmy, sounding puzzled. He craned his neck and looked up at the cross which rose so far above them. "It's not even a gold cross," he said.

Harold looked at Timmy soberly. "It was a cross of shame,"

he said. "And it's what the Lord Jesus did on the cross which is the important thing, not the cross itself."

"He died for us," said Hezekiah.

Timmy looked impatiently at Hezekiah who irritated him so easily.

"This place represents the cross where the Lord Jesus died," explained Harold, "where He died to pay the price for sin so that anyone who trusts in Him can be forgiven of their sins and become a Christian."

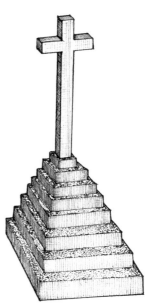

"I know about that," said Timmy. "We have churches at home, you know. My Dad gave loads of money to repair the church steeple in our village. They have a cross there too. Tell them, Jack."

Jack didn't tell them anything. He was gazing at the cross, and at the many steps that led upwards to it, steps that glinted curiously in the sunlight.

"It's because of the chains," Harold explained the glinting

steps. "People leave the chains of sin behind them when they trust in the Lord Jesus. He breaks the chains and sets them free! That's part of the truth of Redemption."

There were so many, many links of chain that formed the smooth steps that led upwards to the cross in the centre of the square. Countless cruel chains that now lay broken and shattered in pieces because the Lord Jesus had paid the awful price of the punishment of sin so that people who trusted in Him didn't have to pay it themselves.

"Well," said Timmy, "I certainly don't have any chains of sin!"

"Everyone has sinned," said Hugo. "The Bible says so[3]!"

"I haven't done much wrong," said Timmy, "nothing like *sin!*"

Hezekiah gasped. He seemed incredulous that Timmy could not see his need. "But you have," he said earnestly. "You have, Barmy, and you need to be saved like anyone else."

Timmy's glance at Hezekiah would have withered the stoutest heart and Hezekiah recoiled as if Timmy had punched him very hard and knocked all of the breath out of him. It wasn't clear what upset Timmy the most: what Hezekiah said about his need to be saved, or his use of the name Barmy, or merely Hezekiah himself. Jack and Hezekiah drew closer together as they followed the others back through the streets of Aletheia and to the Wallops' home once more.

"Timmy's always like that with younger kids," said Jack, seeing Hezekiah's dismayed expression. "He doesn't like me much either."

But Hezekiah's concerns went deeper than the threat of Timmy to his own safety. "He's not saved, Jack," he said. "Imagine not being a Christian!"

That night Jack slept on a comfy bed in the corner of Hezekiah's bedroom. Timmy had a bed in Hugo's room and the large apartment soon settled to the quiet of night. Jack and Hezekiah didn't go quickly to sleep. Into the night Hezekiah whispered and told Jack things about the city of Aletheia and the land of Err. Jack studied a poster of pictures on the wall in Hezekiah's bedroom. They were pictures of the creatures that lived in various parts of Err. They were very strange to Jack, and he wasn't quite sure whether to believe they were real: except that Hezekiah was so certain.

"That's a Glutton," said Hezekiah, looking over Jack's shoulder at the picture of the small, gnome-like creature that was scowling back at them from the poster.

"Have you ever actually seen one?" asked Jack.

Hezekiah sighed. "No," he said regretfully. "We learn about them at school, but not many creatures can get into Aletheia and close to the cross."

"Why?" asked Jack.

"Dad says all bad things are defeated at the cross," said Hezekiah.

"Oh," said Jack.

"Meddlers aren't scary on their own," said Hezekiah, following Jack's continuing examination of the poster. "Don't you have them where you come from?"

"I don't think so," said Jack, suddenly uncertain about this. He thought about the unknown creatures he imagined might live in the big tree outside his bedroom window. Was it possible that Meddlers lived there? He looked closely at the picture of a small, imp-like creature which looked as if it belonged in a children's fairy story. Beside the picture the writing said 'these wicked flying imps stir up trouble and make people quarrel and fight...' The Meddler had small wings on its back and looked mean and spiteful. All the same, Jack was sorry if they didn't exist back home, even if Hezekiah was right about them causing all sorts of problems when they descended in their hosts. But Jack was very glad that the last creature staring at him from Hezekiah's poster did not live in his village: at least he hoped it didn't. It was a terrible monster with vicious teeth and cruel red eyes.

"It's a Wrack," Hezekiah said in hushed, awed tones. "I usually cover up that picture at night."

Jack thought he would too if that monster was on his bedroom wall at home. They both got into their beds and Hezekiah continued to whisper across the darkened bedroom to where Jack lay on the cosy camp bed.

"Don't tell Timmy I cover up the picture of the Wrack," said Hezekiah.

"I won't," promised Jack.

"Timmy might not even believe the Wrack is real," said Hezekiah.

"Timmy doesn't know," said Jack.

"The Wrack lives in the North," whispered Hezekiah. "Right up in the Mountains of Destruction. There are frightening things there that even Captain Steadfast, who has been on missions up there as a Rescuer, won't tell my brother Harold about yet. I think there might be *ghosts* too."

"I don't think ghosts are real," said Jack, reasonably certain about this, "not in my country anyway."

"Well," said Hezekiah after a slight hesitation, "Snares and all the other creatures on my poster are definitely real, and they're scary enough!"

"What do Snares look like exactly?" asked Jack. The poster didn't show much of the Snares. You could only really see their eyes peering from a shapeless shadow.

"No one really knows what they look like," said Hezekiah. "They're wicked, scary, shadowy creatures. They hide in shadows and look like shadows except for their eyes glinting and always watching you! They follow you and try to trap you. And then they take you to terrible places! I bet they even torture you!"

Jack digested this in silence. "Are they everywhere?" he asked at last.

"Oh, they're not right here," said Hezekiah. "At least I don't *think* so," he added more hesitatingly. "They might be in The Outskirts of Aletheia, and they might travel with people who come seeking the Truth, but my Dad says they can't come near the cross, so we're pretty safe here! But if you leave the town, *that's* when they can get you! Of course my Dad says that if you're a Christian and dressed in your armour of salvation, then you can defeat them." Hezekiah paused for a moment. "But even a Christian can be taken by Snares," he concluded solemnly.

"How?" asked Jack.

"I think that it's only if you're not living right as a Christian," said Hezekiah. "I don't know everything about them yet but one day I'm going to be a Rescuer like Ready Steadfast and my brother Harold, and go on missions in Err. Then I'll find out everything for myself! What type of Christian worker do you want to be when you grow up, Jack?"

Jack thought about this in the darkness.

It was easy to think of jobs and other things to be when you were grown up.

But it was harder to think about what *type of Christian* you could turn out to be.

It was very dark when Hezekiah Wallop suddenly awoke with a start. He lay still in the darkness listening intently. From across the bedroom he could hear the steady breathing of peaceful sleep from his new friend Jack Merryweather. He could hear nothing else. Aletheia was still sleeping quietly beneath the night stars and only he was unaccountably awake.

But no!

There it was again: a sudden, faint noise that didn't belong to the calm Aletheian night; a noise that ought not to be there at all. There were faint movements; rustling; scrabbling.

Something was moving about.

The last thing Hezekiah wanted to do was be brave and get out of bed to find out what it was. He searched his mind for options. Could it be a Glutton? Despite what he had said to Jack about no creatures getting close to the cross, did Gluttons get into Aletheia after all? He didn't really know that much about the creatures of Err; most of what he thought he knew came from other children at school who told scary stories about what happened out in the mysterious land of Err and far away from the safety of the cross. Not all the children at school were Christians and some of them had families in Err and still went home to them in the holidays. Was a real, live Glutton moving about in the apartment and placing temptations for the family to fall out over in the morning?

What about a Meddler? Everyone said that they got

everywhere! Surely a Meddler wouldn't dare to come so near to the cross right into his own home and cause trouble here?

But wait: what if some of the creatures of Err were attracted here because of Timmy Trial? Hezekiah didn't know a lot about human behaviour but it didn't take much to see that Timmy had no intention of recognising his need to be set free from his sin and become a Christian. And by his behaviour Timmy probably encouraged all the wicked creatures in Aletheia to come here, right into the safety of the Wallops' home! Hezekiah didn't even want to think what he would do if there was a Snare in the apartment, or if Stumbles now crouched all over the carpeted floor ready to stick to his feet as he walked, making him stumble and fall.

He pulled the quilt right up to his chin and lay very still, willing the strange sound to go away.

It didn't go away.

Something was definitely out there.

But suddenly there was a very human component to the rustling. He distinctly heard someone say "Ow!" very sharply, as if they had just stubbed their toe or hit the funny bone in their elbow. Hezekiah felt a little braver but it was still with some trepidation that he got out of bed and softly crossed to the bedroom door. He wished it wasn't left to him to protect his family and investigate the strange happenings this night. He paused at the bedroom door. His Bible! He needed his Bible! His parents and all the teachers at school always said that a Christian's best weapon was his Bible, so he would take that with him. He fumbled slightly in the darkness as he found it by his bed. Jack Merryweather stirred in his sleep and Hezekiah wished he would wake up, but Jack merely sighed deeply and continued sleeping peacefully.

This time Hezekiah pulled open the bedroom door, crept into the hallway and immediately went towards the kitchen which was close to his bedroom. There was a light on and the noises definitely seemed to be coming from there.

Slowly Hezekiah opened the kitchen door.

CHAPTER 8
TIMMY GOES HIS OWN WAY

Hezekiah stood speechless and astonished in the kitchen doorway. Before him was Timmy Trial, fully dressed in the school uniform he had worn the previous day, with Hugo's jacket over his school shirt as if he was going out for a night stroll. Timmy turned with a startled look to see the small boy observing him and he instantly scowled with anger and annoyance.

"What do you want?" he whispered.

"What are you doing?" asked Hezekiah. It initially appeared to him that Timmy was in the middle of a midnight feast. He was utterly astonished that the big boy could possibly need more to eat than he had already consumed at dinner. But then he noticed that Timmy had a bag that looked a bit like Hugo's old rucksack, and the leftover chocolate cake and biscuits and an assortment of other things that Timmy had found in the kitchen were going into the bag.

"Are you going away?" asked Hezekiah, venturing further into the kitchen.

"It's none of your business," hissed Timmy.

"You can't go away," said Hezekiah, wishing someone else would wake up and help him. "It's too dangerous and Dad said you need to stay near to the cross and learn about how to be saved…"

Timmy moved with surprising suddenness and made a grab at the collar of Hezekiah's pyjamas.

"You're an interfering brat!" he said in a very nasty voice, hoisting Hezekiah clear of the floor and squeezing his neck, "and if you make one more noise or say one more word I'll break your neck!"

There was no doubt at that moment that Timmy would have needed little provocation to do just that. As it was he gave Hezekiah a big shove and sent him flying onto the floor and clattering into a cupboard.

"I didn't make that noise!" panted Hezekiah. "You did it when you knocked me into the cupboard so you can't break my neck for that!"

There was something about the small boy, pale and frightened, in his pyjamas, and now sprawled on the kitchen floor, that utterly infuriated Timmy Trial. He aimed a kick at Hezekiah and there was a yelp of protest.

"You made me make that noise too!" said Hezekiah. "You can't blame that on me!"

"Shut up!" demanded Timmy. "Just shut up!"

Hezekiah got slowly to his feet as Timmy hastily shoved the remaining food within his reach into the old rucksack and prepared to leave.

"I don't think you should be taking all that food," said Hezekiah. He hastily backed away at the look on Timmy's face. "I mean, Mum wouldn't want you to be hungry or anything, but I don't think you should just take it all without even asking…"

He was cornered by Timmy who once more hoisted him up from the floor by his collar.

"SHUT UP!" said Timmy, trying to keep his own voice to a whisper but wanting nothing more than to yell at this unforeseen and most unwelcome interference. "If you don't shut up…!"

"Alright!" Hezekiah choked out, and he was dropped unceremoniously onto the floor where he rubbed at his neck ruefully. But as he watched Timmy's preparations for departure

Hezekiah could not remain silent. He got slowly to his feet again.

"But where are you going?" he asked. "I mean, you might need help, you might need to be rescued and then we need to know where to find you and…" Hezekiah trailed away as Timmy towered over him, glowering and furious.

"I have friends here, brat," Timmy hissed in his face, "and I have plans that don't include *you!*"

Hezekiah shrank from Timmy as if he was preparing himself for a punch from Timmy's big fist. But he didn't run away, and bravely he held out the Bible he clutched tightly in his hand. "I think you should take this with you," he said.

Timmy's face was a picture of fury and awful uncertainty. His conscience was smitten, but he would not yield to this boy who dared to challenge him and who quite unexpectedly made him doubt. He wanted to get away from Aletheia; he wanted to meet up with Wonky Dollar as he'd arranged; he wanted opportunities and riches and importance, none of which was here. He was going to make the most of the discovery of this strange, unknown land. He would not return home empty handed.

"Go back to bed," whispered Timmy in a spluttering, half

choking sort of way. "And just be glad I didn't give you the beating you deserve!"

The apartment was once again silent and Hezekiah stood in the hallway looking at the front door that had just clicked shut behind Timmy Trial. Still no one else seemed to stir. He returned to his bedroom feeling defeated and worried at what he should do next, but when he opened the door he could see Jack Merryweather's form sitting up in bed.

"Zek?" Jack asked uncertainly.

Hezekiah came into the room and sat down on his own bed, flicking on his bedside light and placing his Bible back in its place. "Timmy's gone," he said without preamble.

"Gone?"

"Gone into Err," said Hezekiah in a solemn tone.

Jack wasn't sure why that was such a bad thing, but he knew enough from Hezekiah's concern to realise that somehow Timmy wasn't safe; and besides, how would Timmy find his way home again to Grandad's sheds and school if he went further away from the way they had come in? It was a sobering thought.

"What shall we do?" asked Jack.

"I don't know," said Hezekiah.

"Should we tell your Dad?" ventured Jack.

"Perhaps we should wake Hugo," said Hezekiah. "He'll know what to do, and he might have noticed that Timmy is missing."

Hugo had not noticed the absence of Timmy from the camp bed in his bedroom. He had slept peacefully through the entire episode and it took some time for the two younger boys to rouse Hugo sufficiently to understand what had just occurred.

"Let's get Henry," said Hugo.

A short while later the four of them, Hugo and Henrietta, Jack and Hezekiah, stood on the outside balcony of the Wallops' high apartment overlooking the quiet, dark city of Aletheia. The dim light of very early dawn began to show at the edges of the horizon, like daylight stealing through a crack in the curtains. Through Mr Wallop's telescope on the balcony they took it in turns to scan the city and the land which they could see to the south and the east. There

was little movement in Aletheia this early in the morning and it didn't take them too long to spy a lone figure that they decided must be Timmy, walking south down Apathy Road. They kept the telescope on Timmy as he neared the boundary of the city and crossed the Water of Sound Doctrine. And then Timmy went on into the land of Err.

It was the very earliest hours of Saturday and Aletheia was still asleep. Only the four children on the balcony were awake and, in the whispered discussion regarding what they should do about Timmy's disappearance, one plan was clearly favoured.

"We'll go after him of course," said Henrietta.

"Into Err?" asked Hezekiah in awe.

"I don't know, Henry," said Hugo, who was far more cautious than his twin.

"If we go now…"

"In our pyjamas?" asked Hezekiah.

"No, Zek," said Henrietta in her most patient manner, "we'll dress of course, and just slip out and overtake him!"

"We'll need armour," said Hugo.

"Well, of course!" responded Henrietta.

"And supplies."

"We won't be gone long!"

"I don't know what Dad and Mum would say..."

"But it's them we're thinking about!" said Henrietta eagerly. "Saturday is the only day they get any rest. We can't wake them now and we'll be back before they've even had their morning coffee!"

"I don't think Timmy will want to come back," said Jack.

"We don't even know where Timmy is heading," said Hugo.

"Down Apathy Road, obviously," said Henrietta. "And if we hurry then we'll see him on the road before he gets too far!"

"Is there a place called Wishy-Washy?" asked Jack.

"Yes!" exclaimed Henrietta.

"Wishy-Washy is famous for its Fair," said Hugo. "They have one most Saturdays."

"When Timmy was whispering with Mr Dollar I think I overheard him mentioning Wishy-Washy," said Jack. "Do you think they could be meeting there?"

"More than likely," said Henrietta. "They really could be you know, Hugo!" she added to her sceptical twin.

"What else did they say?" Hugo asked Jack.

"I didn't catch that much," admitted Jack, "but I think there was something about a fortune teller, or making a fortune…"

"There!" cried Henrietta. "They're going to Wishy-Washy Fair! They have all kinds of fortune telling and other stuff there. I expect that Wonky Dollar was heading to the Fair and told Timmy to meet him there!"

"It's not exactly a hundred percent certain that they're going there, Henry," said Hugo drily.

"We'll leave a note to explain to Mum and Dad where we're going," said Henrietta. "That way they'll know where to find us if…well, if they really need to. Come on, we must hurry!"

The note for their parents was the subject of some whispered disputing between Hugo and Henrietta. But in the end the need for haste made them keep it short and to the point, and it simply said: '*Gone to find Timmy who we think has run away to Wishy-Washy Fair. Don't worry, we'll be back soon.*' They left the note propped up by the empty coffee pot in the kitchen where their

parents were certain to find it.

"I don't think that they won't worry just because we say so," said Hugo as they scanned the note one final time.

But a hint of light peeping out of the bottom of the grey, dawn sky sent them scurrying on their way: for if they were to find Timmy and return triumphant before their parents started to worry, they needed to do it soon.

They fitted Jack with spare armour from the hallway cupboard. Jack was sorry that they were unable to go to the main Armoury of Aletheia which the others explained was at the Academy of Soldiers-of-the-Cross. He imagined the rows of armour and real soldiers that might be there; he hoped they might visit there another time. But Henrietta was telling them all to hurry and Jack quickly fastened the pieces of armour that Hugo handed to him.

"We need all the armour for protection," said Hugo.

Jack wondered what he needed protecting against. All those creatures on the poster in Hezekiah's bedroom for sure, and what else might there be out there in the land of Err…?

"The Bible[6] is our only weapon of attack," explained Hezekiah, watching Jack finish putting on his armour and tucking the Bible safely into the pouch at his side, "All the other bits…" he pointed at the belt, the body armour, the boots, the shield strapped on his back, and his helmet, "the other bits are for protection. I'm not exactly sure how it works in your country…?" he sounded slightly apologetic at this fact. It was clearly puzzling to the Wallop children that Jack was a Christian and yet he had never worn armour like this before.

"I'm not exactly sure how it works either," said Jack. "But I think it might be that our armour is completely invisible to everyone."

Hezekiah nodded reassuringly. "Yes," he said, "I expect that's it. Dad says that our seventh bit of armour is prayer and that's invisible too, isn't it?"

Jack thought about what Mr Wallop had said about Mr Duffle and how his prayers were of great benefit[7]. He wondered if old Mr Duffle was praying today. It was a strange thought that something like prayer, that was so silent and invisible, was so powerful. Nobody could see it, and you could pray silently, or out loud, anytime, anyplace; and yet it could make such a difference in a battle, or a difficult situation, or just in the small, everyday things of life. It was because God was listening; and God could do anything.

"Dad says it's possible to put on your armour with your mind," said Hezekiah. "Maybe that's how it works in your country."

Jack thought that Hezekiah was right. He was certain that the armour of God was just as important for a Christian back home, away from Aletheia. And while at home there might be snares which could take over people and cause them to turn away from God, in the land of Err the things that trapped a Christian might be visible, frightening, terrible creatures!

There was a bird singing as they stepped into the greyness of early dawn. Jack was pleased how comfortable the armour felt. It was easy and light to wear and it seemed to keep him warm despite the early morning chill.

They met no one as they moved through the narrow, crooked streets of Aletheia that the Wallop children knew so well. They walked quickly and almost in silence by the cross where one lone star, the morning star, still twinkled brightly above them.

Then they hurried away from the city centre and down Apathy Road where Timmy had gone only a short while before. This was a smooth, straight, gently sloping road that was quick and easy. And before they knew it they had reached The Outskirts of Aletheia and the bridge over the wide, dark, swirling Water of Sound Doctrine that marked the boundary of the city.

They were about to enter the land of Err.

CHAPTER 9
WISHY-WASHY FAIR

The group of four paused for a moment at the bridge that spanned the deep, fast current that was the Water of Sound Doctrine and that marked the boundary of the city of Aletheia. They leaned over the stone parapet and looked into the water that ran so swiftly beneath them. There were rainbow colours and sparkles and swirls and a thousand different diamonds sparkling in it even in the greyness of dawn.

"No one knows how deep it is," said Hezekiah.

"No one has ever managed to plumb the depths of the water," explained Hugo.

"No one can ever drink too much of it," added Henrietta.

They were all carrying water bottles from the Wallops' apartment. Jack didn't like to think what would happen if they ran out. To drink anything but the crystal water that now flowed beneath them seemed unthinkable.

Nothing remarkable happened when they stepped off the bridge and started down the gently sloping Apathy Road into Err. The dawn was still grey and there were patches of trees and hedges and thickets along the side of the road. The first person that they saw was a man setting up the outdoor bargain tables at the Recycle Centre not far from Aletheia. He was putting books into piles and setting out DVDs and posters and other things on the tables for sale or exchange.

"Good morning," said Hugo politely.

"Good morning, young man!" the man said, stopping what he was doing. "You're very early customers!" He was a cheerful man with a big head, lots of chins, and an enormous stomach.

"Well, actually," said Hugo, "we're not really customers."

"Never mind," said the man. "I'm afraid I couldn't really give you too much in exchange for your Bibles anyway; there's really not much market for the old fashioned ones these days. People are far more interested in books that they can really understand; books that can really help them with the issues of life, you see?"

"No," said Hugo.

"The Bible *can* really help them!" said Henrietta.

The man smiled. "Ah, loyal Aletheians," he said. "Well, I doubt there's much I can tempt you with here!"

"No, thank you," said Hugo.

"Is that man a Christian?" Jack whispered to Hezekiah. The

two smaller boys drew aside and examined the old fashioned Bibles on the 'Buy One Get Two Free' table.

"He might be," said Hezekiah. "I know some Christians live in Err, I think I've heard it's because they don't want the whole truth of the Bible, just the bits they like the best, you know?"

The Recycle Centre man was talking to Hugo and Henrietta as he set out another box of books which had 'About Self' stamped on the outside of the box. "Believe it or not, you're not my first callers today!" he said. "There was another boy who came by when I was having my morning coffee. Knocked on the door, he did, I nearly spilt my coffee! I don't usually get customers come by before light but this boy seemed to like the look of my poster advertising the 'Get-Rich-Quick' schemes and had a look at some books and things."

"That'll be Barmy!" said Henrietta.

"Barmy?" said the man. "I don't think that was his name."

"Definitely Barmy," agreed Hugo.

"Anyway, he exchanged some chocolate cake he had for a couple of things…" the man said.

"The little thief!" exclaimed Henrietta.

The man didn't seem to understand what Henrietta meant.

"Mind you," the man said, "I don't think the chocolate cake will last long; it doesn't have the right preservatives in it."

"Well! Of all the…!" began Henrietta.

Hugo placed a firm hand on her arm.

"He's lucky he got away with the book and DVD he wanted before I found out the cake was already sinking in the middle!" the man said.

"It's made with Pray-Always farmland ingredients!" Henrietta said indignantly. "It'll never last out here!"

"You may be right," the man said. "It needs more artificial preservatives in it. Well, I'll eat it with my coffee before it's wasted!"

Hugo restrained his sister from insisting on the return of Mrs Wallop's chocolate cake that Timmy had pilfered from their kitchen. "Let him have it, Henry," he murmured as the man was distracted straightening some DVDs.

"It's not as if he needs it!" protested Henrietta as they said goodbye and walked away. "Did you see the size of his tummy?!"

Hezekiah giggled.

"I really don't know," continued Henrietta as they walked on down the road, "I don't know whether I'll punch Barmy or preach at him when I see him! Stealing food from the kitchen indeed! I thought there weren't many leftovers when I grabbed some food for us! You're really very good not to tell tales about what happened in the kitchen, Zek," she continued to her youngest brother, "but Barmy Bats is in deep trouble when I see him!"

"We're supposed to be helping him, Henry," said Hugo.

Henrietta sighed. "Well, once he's apologised I suppose we'll help him too," she said.

The further they walked the higher the sun rose and the thicker and heavier the air became. On Apathy Road there was nothing of the cool, crystal clarity of the air around the cross in Aletheia, but the odd thing was that the helmets that they wore had a soothing effect in the heat. It was as if the helmet carried with it some of the refreshing air which was always around the cross high on the hill now behind them. There were still trees and shrubs and hedges lining the road. In one prickly thicket Jack thought he saw a mysterious shadow. It was the merest hint of *something* that wasn't quite *nothing* hidden behind thick leaves at the side of the road. It didn't seem possible that it was actually something real; it didn't seem possible that the glittering eyes he saw were *watching them* and that it could be a real, live Snare.

"I think I saw it too!" agreed Hezekiah. "Is it a Snare? That's the first real Snare I've ever seen! Do you think it really could be…?" His hand was tightly clutching his Bible.

"I think it's just normal shadows, Zek," said Henrietta.

"We're fine as long as we keep our armour on," said Hugo.

But Jack saw both of the twins looking furtively around them and he wondered if Hugo and Henrietta were really as certain as they seemed.

After a while they all got used to shadows and the grey dawn turned steadily to the light of day. The air was warm, and the sun began to rise, beckoning the start of another hot, summer day. All was still and safe and tranquil. There was no danger in sight.

They heard the noise of music and people before they turned the final corner on Apathy Road and came to Wishy-Washy. The air had grown so warm and thick that there was a haze of cloud hanging over the town. It made everything seem distant and colourless, as if someone had poured a bucket of water over Wishy-Washy and all the colours in the buildings and the people had run thin and mostly been washed away. On the edge of the town, in a big open field by the side of Apathy Road, there was the Wishy-Washy Fair. 'Welcome!' declared a big sign, and, 'Fair for Fundraising for Good and Desirable Causes' another said. It wasn't exactly clear what the Fair supported but it sounded nice enough.

It was still early in the morning when they arrived at the Fair but behind the layers of misty cloud the sun was already creeping up in the sky. Hugo was wondering how on earth they would accomplish their mission and return to the Wallops' apartment without their parents missing them. He was beginning to anticipate the frustrating adult type questions that would inevitably ensue and to which they might not, after all, have an acceptable answer. Henrietta was still optimistic about their parents' attitude towards the mission they had undertaken, and besides, she reasoned, they were here now, they would have to make the most of it. They made their way into the Fair and started exploring the part of Wishy-Washy Fair which was closest to them, silently dismayed at its size and how many rows of tents and stalls and marquees and even caravans and animal enclosures that there were. There were refreshment stalls too and, since they had imprudently demolished the remainder of their picnic on first arrival at Wishy-Washy, they looked with great temptation at the ice-cream and hot dogs and burgers and chips and other tantalising treats that were being set up as they wandered around.

"How will we find Timmy?" asked Hezekiah. He was not overly concerned with this problem since he was certain one of the twins had an answer that wasn't apparent to him. Both he and Jack were far more anxious about what they would eat.

"We just keep looking," said Henrietta.

And wearily, grimly, with increasing impatience and hunger, they looked.

Jack and Hezekiah began to flag by the time they considered it must be lunchtime. Hugo was increasingly gloomy about their prospects of coming out of the whole venture with even the smallest credit, and Henrietta was doggedly determined to prove they were right in coming and by hook or by crook still hoped to find Timmy.

And it was in this state that they found Mr and Mrs Weighty.

Actually Mr and Mrs Weighty were not at all hard to find. They had a stall at the fair which was bright and cheery and stood out through the hazy air as if it had not suffered the same fate as the rest of Wishy-Washy. Whoever might have washed the colour away from Wishy-Washy had certainly not managed to rinse the 'Whole Truth' stall that Moore and Truly Weighty ran. They appeared to be the only undiluted colour in the whole place and the four weary travellers were drawn to the stall with some relief.

A huge, burly man with a massive bushy beard and a bright orange bowtie was arranging Bibles and leaflets on the stall. He turned quickly when he heard Hezekiah's exclamation of "Look, Hugo – Bibles!"

"Ah! The wanderers from Aletheia!" the big man said with an encouraging smile. He sounded as if he knew them. "Well, this is very nice! Very nice indeed! Did they send you with more Bibles and bottled Water of Sound Doctrine and the supplies of leaflets that I asked for? No…?" he laughed heartily, a deep, contagious, ringing laugh. "I'm only teasing," he said. "I can see you haven't come with much!" he clapped Hugo on the back. "Now, you all come in for a nice hot breakfast," he said. "And then we'll see what we can do!"

"I thought it was lunchtime!" Hezekiah said

candidly, and Mr Weighty chuckled again.

"I'm glad you're found," he said. "You saved me coming to search for you!"

They all sat around the ample camp table that Mrs Weighty had in a private part of the big tent which was their stall. Mr and Mrs Weighty, who were the Outpost Rescuers in the part of Err where Wishy-Washy was, explained that they had received word from the Wallops in Aletheia that the children were on their way to the Fair.

"Oh," groaned Hugo.

"Well, at least we left them that note, Hugo," said Henrietta. "They must be pleased about that!"

Jack wondered how people received word over a distance in Aletheia. "Do you have telephones?" he asked, trying to recall whether he had seen such a thing in the Wallops' apartment.

"Telephone?" echoed Mr Weighty, sounding puzzled.

"He's from a different country," said Hezekiah.

"Ah," said Mr Weighty. "Well, young man," he explained, "here we have our Mission Detector system which connects all the Outpost Rescuers in Err with the folk in Aletheia."

"Oh," said Jack. He didn't think it polite to tell Mr Weighty he had no idea what he was talking about.

Hugo and Henrietta were pretty mortified that the Weightys, who were busy Christian workers trying to help people in Err, had been notified of their disappearance, and even Henrietta was no longer optimistic that their original plan might be viewed with approval.

"They'll only see the bad bits," she said sadly. "They only ever see the bits that go wrong!"

Hezekiah was less concerned about the fallout from their adventure. His most pressing concern, which was their risk of starving in Err or eating the wrong food, had happily passed. He wondered what would have happened if he had succumbed to the ice-cream he had found tempting at the Fair. Would it have made him do dreadful, unchristian-type things?

"It's not a good idea," said Mr Weighty, when Hezekiah asked him about it. "Because basically what you take in from around here has usually been watered down or added to or altered in some way, and so it will start to affect your appreciation of the Truth. So if you're eating food that isn't watered by the Water of Sound Doctrine and grown on the Pray-Always farms, then you will begin to get a taste for things that aren't quite what the

Bible says. It might be small things to start with, but it's wise to avoid anything that will affect your appreciation of the whole Truth of the Bible. Do you see?"

Hezekiah wasn't certain he did see exactly what Mr Weighty meant but he gave a sort-of nod quite politely. It didn't sound quite as bad as he feared but he was still very glad they had the food that the Weightys had lavishly provided.

"Why is everything so washed out around here?" asked Jack. "I don't think there's much colour at all, except for here of course."

"Well," said Mr Weighty, "it's really because people have watered down everything. There are Christians here who have watered down the Truth of the Bible or just chosen the bits they like and so have become all watery and wishy-washy about what they believe. And there are people who aren't Christians who don't mind some bits of the Bible but sadly have never grasped the whole Truth and come to the Lord Jesus to be saved. That's why everything has become misty and unclear, because that's what these people are. Does that help?"

Jack nodded. It was an intriguing idea: that places became like the people who lived there. He wondered what his own village would look like if it imitated what the people were on the inside.

"You must be careful to stick to the whole, balanced Truth of the Bible," said Mr Weighty, "then you can be exactly what God wants you to be."

Mr and Mrs Weighty were altogether very kind to them and listened seriously to their account of the runaway Timmy and their mission to find him. They didn't say obvious, adult things, like the fact that they really should have woken their parents when they realised Timmy was missing. They didn't lecture them on the rule about always going into Err accompanied by a mature Christian. They didn't even mention the fact that they should have notified the official Rescuer on duty of the missing Timmy and left the rescue to the people who knew how to do these things properly. Instead they plied the hungry travellers with hot buttered toast, and sausages and eggs cooked on Mrs Weighty's special camp stove.

"Your brother Harold is coming to get you later today," Mr Weighty informed them when they had eaten so much they felt they could burst at the seams.

"Oh!" said Henrietta, pleased.

"At least it's Harold," said Hugo. Their oldest brother might well say more than Mr Weighty on the subject of their ill-conceived morning journey, but Harold was pretty understanding too.

"Does that mean we get to stay at the Fair until Harold comes?" asked Henrietta.

Mr Weighty nodded. "And stay out of trouble too, we hope!" he said with a smile.

Jack and Hezekiah could hardly keep their eyes open after their big breakfast with the Weightys. They had, after all, been up since the small, dark hours of the night. Mrs Weighty made the boys a comfy bed with blankets and rugs in the corner of the private bit of the tent.

And before the sun was at its highest in the sky, the two boys were sound asleep.

CHAPTER 10
THE PROPHECIES OF WANDER PALM

It was very quiet in the tent when Jack awoke. He felt wide awake and, as he sat up, Hezekiah also stirred and opened his eyes.

"Where are we...Oh!" said Hezekiah, "I thought I might have dreamt it all but it's really true! We came to Wishy-Washy Fair!"

Jack nodded. He wondered if the whole thing: Aletheia, Err, and Wishy-Washy Fair and even his friend Hezekiah and the rest of the Wallops too might all be a dream. But it seemed real enough: getting out of the blankets, putting on his armour boots, following Hezekiah to the tent door.

The adjoining stall was silent. The lines of Bibles and neat piles of leaflets were still there, as was the chair that Mrs Weighty usually sat in, with a roll of brightly coloured knitting just where she had left it. They looked around the empty stall and discovered a note pinned to the front of the stall for people that were passing. 'Back in five minutes' it said.

They didn't discuss it much; they just walked slowly out of the Whole Truth stall into the swirling mist and lively excitement of Wishy-Washy Fair. There were plenty of people now, far more than earlier, and they thronged around the stalls and stood chatting in clusters and laughed and called to each other.

The two boys didn't go too far, just as far as a big tent with sports stuff like footballs and cricket bats with sayings and verses printed on them. The sayings were all about God and being nice. There was a pair of 'gospel trainers' on special sale and sports T-shirts with a 'Run the Race and Win' logo on the front. They were examining a football with 'Play Fair, Win Square' printed on it when they heard an unmistakable voice. First Jack and then Hezekiah peered around a very large lady who was browsing through the 'bargain' Christmas cards close by.

Sure enough, there was Timmy Trial!

Timmy was not alone. He wasn't with Wonky Dollar, but instead he had three big boys crowding around him and he was trying to explain to them how much money he had left to spend. Jack knew that he was trying to impress the big boys: in fact, it was almost as if Timmy was a bit afraid of them.

"I thought you had enough for a football so we could have a game," the biggest boy said.

"We spent quite a bit of money in the food tent," said Timmy.

"They're from Topsy-Turvy Progressive School!" Hezekiah whispered in Jack's ear.

Jack shrugged. "What's that?" he asked.

"It's the worst school in Err!" said Hezekiah. "They're awful there! Everything is done the opposite way around: so the kids are in charge and make all the rules!"

"Wow," said Jack. He couldn't even imagine how a school like that might work, but he could see that the three lads that had somehow become friends with Timmy looked even more like bullies than Timmy did himself!

"We've got to help Timmy," said Hezekiah.

"Right," said Jack, wanting to do nothing of the sort.

Both boys hesitated. They did *not* want to approach the bigger boys, but what if they lost Timmy again? In the end the large lady looking at the Christmas cards decided it. She looked down at them and their whispered conversation with a disgruntled, disagreeable expression on her face.

"Are you buying Christmas cards?" she asked abruptly.

"Uh, no thanks," Jack said, thinking that fact was abundantly obvious.

"Well, then," said the lady. "If you wouldn't mind *moving*…"

"Oh, sorry," said Hezekiah, and the two boys reluctantly moved from their safe hiding place.

Timmy was staring in their direction when they emerged. Probably he had heard their voices.

"What are you doing here?" he demanded with a glance of concern at his big friends.

"Who are they?" one of the Topsy-Turvy boys sneered.

"Do they come from your country?" another asked. "Do they have any of your country's money on them?"

"We've been trying to find you, Barmy!" exclaimed Hezekiah.

One of the boys thumped Timmy on the back and gave a roar of laughter. "The little squirt just called you *Barmy*!" he said.

"Are you going to stand for that?" another said.

"Excuse me!" the big lady said as she tried to manoeuvre around them again to look at the 'I Love Angels' bracelets.

The two smaller boys moved reluctantly out of her way and closer to Timmy and the other big boys.

Timmy's face was red and then purple as he fixed on Hezekiah who was looking bemused and then most alarmed. "I was only trying to say..." he began.

Timmy took hold of one of Hezekiah's ears and began to squeeze it hard between his fingers.

Hezekiah gave a squeal of agony and the big boys laughed.

"Leave him alone!" said Jack.

"Let's see if they've got any money!" one of the bully boys said.

"Leave him alone!" Jack said again, and shoved Timmy as hard as he could.

It was unfortunate that Timmy was unbalanced at that moment. Usually Jack shoving Timmy would have no effect whatsoever, but this time he went reeling into the rack of bargain Christmas cards and crashing to the ground. In the confusion that followed – Timmy's roar of rage, the equally loud roar of encouragement of the big boys, the shout of the man who ran the stall, the squeal of protest from the fat lady who seemed to be trapped in the middle of them again – through all this Jack was not slow to respond. He grabbed Hezekiah and together the two of them ducked through the back of the stall and ran as if their lives depended on it.

Jack had the vague idea that he and Hezekiah were running in the direction of the Weightys' stall but he knew, when they had run for some time, that somewhere they had missed the way. They ducked and dived and weaved through what seemed like countless avenues of stalls and tents. All the time they ran he could hear the sounds of Timmy and the other boys shouting and pursuing and at last he and Hezekiah ducked behind a purple tent and stopped to catch their breath.

"What shall we do?" whispered Hezekiah.

"We can outrun them I think," said Jack. "Otherwise…"

"Otherwise they'll get us," said Hezekiah. "And there are four of them!"

Cautiously Jack stuck his head around the side of the strange purple tent. "I think it's just Timmy," he whispered. It appeared that the other boys, perhaps having spent Timmy's money and grown tired of Timmy himself, had abandoned him somewhere during the pursuit. Jack watched Timmy come to a stop, clutching his sides and panting and looking with interest at the purple tent behind which Jack and Hezekiah were hidden. It was a strange tent, and Jack realised they had escaped to the outskirts of the Fair where the grey mist was thicker even than before and where the sun seemed barely to shine. No longer were they close to stalls which sold trinkets that said 'Smile! God Loves You!' and had nice pictures for sale with sayings that, even if they weren't exactly in the Bible, seemed to mean good things. Here the stalls were more secluded and mysterious. Opposite to where they were hidden Jack could see a 'Spiritual Tattoos' tent which didn't look very nice at all. And there were definitely shadows that reminded Jack of what Hezekiah had said about Snares. He was about to say so when he heard a woman's voice.

"Are you coming in?" she asked. She had a calm, deep voice and it seemed she was talking to Timmy.

"Umm…are you Mrs Palm who does the prophecies?" asked Timmy.

"It's Ms Palm actually," the lady said, and they saw her now emerging slowly from the front of the tent to face Timmy. "And yes, I am the Wander Palm of 'Wander Palm's Prophetic Mystery Telling,'" and she gestured to the sign above her purple tent.

She was a tall lady and she was swathed in black and deep

purple which matched the tent. Jack didn't need Hezekiah's frantic whisper in his ear to realise that the appearance of the lady was not particularly reassuring.

"We've got to warn Timmy," said Hezekiah. "I don't think this can be right at all!"

"Umm…I think I heard about you from my…umm, friend… Wonky Dollar," said Timmy.

"Mr Dollar was here earlier," the lady said. "He found my prophecies most relevant to his future needs!"

"Is prophesying in the Bible?" Jack whispered to Hezekiah.

"I think so," said Hezekiah sounding perplexed, "but I still don't think this is right!"

"Perhaps it's not the whole Truth of the Bible, like Mr Weighty warned us," said Jack. "Perhaps she's just pretending because she's heard of prophecies in the Bible or something."

"I was supposed to meet Wonky at the Fair," said Timmy. "Do you know where he was going…?"

"He was going to meet his future with fortitude," the lady said mysteriously.

"What on earth does that mean?" whispered Hezekiah.

"I don't think it means anything!" said Jack.

"Come in, young man," the lady said to Timmy in a deep, mysterious voice. "I won't bite, you know, you need not look so cautious! My prophecies are a Bible gift!"

"I don't have much money left," Timmy was saying to the lady. He held out a handful of coins and the lady picked up one and looked at it closely.

"I haven't seen money like this before," she said, clearly impressed. "You can have a few minutes of prophecy for this. You do have such a promising face!"

"Do I?" said Timmy, looking pleased.

Jack and Hezekiah glanced at each other. Anyone who told Timmy that he had a promising face either needed their eyesight tested or their prophetic ability examined.

"See!" murmured Hezekiah. "It can't be right!"

Jack agreed. But really what could they do…?

"We'll wait for Timmy," he decided. "And take him back to the Weightys with us."

"Can you really tell me about the future?" Timmy asked the lady as he followed her into the tent.

"I can examine your prospects," the lady said ambiguously.

Timmy and the lady vanished and Hezekiah beckoned Jack

to a small hole in the side of the purple tent where they could peep in and watch Timmy have his future told.

Jack had never seen someone trying to tell the future before. It was pretty odd. The lady was examining Timmy's head as if he was being checked for head lice when there was an outbreak at school. She was telling him that he would one day grow very tall and strong and might even be a great man in Err. How she got all that through Timmy's untidy, uncombed and probably even unwashed hair was maybe the *mystery* bit of Wander Palm's Prophecies.

"Will I be rich?" asked Timmy.

"You have gold prospects," the lady said soothingly in her mesmerising voice.

"Umm…does that mean I'll be rich?" asked Timmy.

Hezekiah bit back a sudden giggle.

"She's just saying anything," Jack whispered in disgust. "It's just as well that Timmy doesn't understand her!"

"Will I make money in Err by catching it from the sky?" asked Timmy.

"Many have tried and the chosen few will succeed," the lady said impressively.

There was a pause in which Timmy screwed up his face and evidently tried to figure out whether he would, or would not, succeed in making his fortune in the land of Err.

"And umm…will I go back home soon?" asked Timmy.

"Home?" the lady considered. "Ah, but where is home?" she asked as if there was something deep and meaningful about it.

"Home to England," explained Timmy. "That's where I live…"

"I thought that you lived in a country called Grandad's Sheds?" Hezekiah whispered to Jack.

Jack shook his head, concentrating on the scene inside the tent. "He shouldn't have told her that," he hissed. "She thinks he's from Err somewhere! She doesn't actually know anything!"

"Yes, yes," the lady said, "England. Soon loved ones will be reunited once more…"

"How do I get there exactly?" asked Timmy.

The lady hesitated. "Our way will be clear before us when it shall be revealed," she said in a most significant tone.

Jack had suddenly had enough. "What rot!" he said to Hezekiah. "That doesn't really mean anything at all!"

The lady's head snapped around and Timmy was staring open-mouthed at the tent wall.

"Who's there?" the lady said sternly as if she was talking to something invisible.

There was a pause in which Hezekiah tightly clutched Jack's arm, and then:

"A spirit from the future is here," Jack droned in a strange, unearthly voice.

Hezekiah started suddenly and pinched Jack's arm. "What are you doing?" he hissed wildly.

Jack shook his head at him, putting a finger to his lips.

"Timmy Trial must leave at once!" he said in the same oddly detached voice which was most unlike his own.

The lady's face went very white, and then very red. Timmy seemed utterly bereft of speech.

"Who are you…?" faltered the lady.

"Leave at once Timmy Trial," said the unearthly voice. "Or more doom will befall you!"

Timmy got suddenly from his chair and staggered slightly as he stood.

The lady stood too. "I don't think it's anything to worry about," she said to Timmy, but Jack heard the awful uncertainty in her voice. "This has never happened before. It might be a special revelation…"

Jack hadn't thought of what to do next; he was utterly astonished that his pretence had been remotely believable. He decided to continue.

"Your friends are waiting for you!" he intoned in the same ghostly voice. "Come out Timmy Trial! Come out Timmy Trial!"

Hezekiah gave a sudden, helpless splutter of hysterical laughter.

And instantly the spell was broken.

With an unearthly, frightening cry of rage the lady moved swiftly from the back of the tent and around the corner before the two boys could think to flee.

"You wicked, wicked boys!" she yelled. "How dare you say those things! How dare you…!" The deep mysterious voice and the dignity were gone, and the wild look in her eyes gave her a terrifying appearance.

"You were making things up too!" Jack said desperately. His bold words were certainly true but they were unlikely to sooth the outraged woman in the black and purple robes. Hezekiah grabbed his arm and once more the two of them were on the run.

And once again Timmy was in hot pursuit.

CHAPTER 11
A NIGHT IN THE FOREST

This time, as they fled through the Fair, they were glad that Timmy followed them. They just needed to get away from the angry, scary Wander Palm and back to the safety of the Weightys' Whole Truth tent. For a few moments Jack and Hezekiah thought that their adventures might be over; that at any moment they would round a corner or slip through another narrow tented alleyway and find the splash of colour that was the Weightys' stall. And this time they would have Timmy with them.

But when they did stop it was not at the safety of the Weightys' stall. They had reached the outskirts of the Fair, the tents and caravans and stalls were now behind them, and in the distance, through the haze, they could see the rooftops of the town of Wishy-Washy. Timmy came running up behind them and slid to a stop, panting heavily and staring at them both. For a moment they all looked at each other in silence; for a moment it seemed that Timmy had forgotten why he had been chasing them.

"I ought to give you both a sound beating," he said at last.

"Your friends are gone," said Hezekiah.

"I could deal with you very well on my own!" said Timmy.

"There are two of us," said Jack.

For a second it seemed as though Timmy was going to launch himself at both of them, but his expression subsided into something like weary acceptance.

"Ms Palm has probably put a spell on you for what you did," he said darkly.

"She certainly looked like a witch," said Jack. "But I don't think she knew much."

Timmy looked annoyed at that and Hezekiah hastily intervened.

"Anyway, we really were looking for you, you know," he said.

"I can look after myself," said Timmy.

Indeed, he didn't look as if he had done too badly since he had left the Wallops home very early that morning. He wore a new light-weight rain jacket which had the logo 'Love Yourself' on the pocket and new 'designer' trainers too. He still had Hugo's old rucksack slung on his back and it appeared to have plenty inside it; but Timmy had nearly run out of money now.

Jack looked at Timmy. "What are you going to do now?" he asked.

It had never seriously occurred to any of the Wallop children that Timmy might refuse to return with them to Aletheia; only Jack had wondered how and if they would be able to persuade him to return. Timmy looked around them, at the distant rooftops of Wishy-Washy in the mist ahead, and behind them at the Fair. They had not noticed it until now but the mist which had been light and hazy earlier had turned thick and damp and grey. The sun had vanished and a light drizzle of rain was beginning to fall.

Hezekiah was in no doubt what to do next. "We'll go and have tea with the Weightys!" he said.

Surprisingly Timmy, perhaps through lack of any other ideas, or maybe with the hope of tea in mind, followed the two smaller boys as they began to walk vaguely in the direction that they thought must lead to the Weightys' stall. They were surprised to see that the Fair appeared to be over and that tents were being packed away. Streams of people were leaving the Fair and the three boys joined the mass of moving people and trudged through the increasing gloom and steady drizzle of rain. It seemed that at any moment they would reach the side of the Fair where the

Weightys had their stall.

"I think the Weightys' stall was on the side of the Fair near Apathy Road," said Hezekiah.

"This is stupid," grumbled Timmy. "They've probably gone home by now!"

Jack approached a lady who was walking close by and seemed to know where she was going. "Excuse me, is this the way to Apathy Road?" he asked.

"Oh, I dare say it is if you want it to be," the lady said.

"What does that mean?" asked Timmy. But the lady had passed by and was quickly lost to sight through the mist and rain.

"Excuse me," Hezekiah tried to stop a man who was hurrying on his way, no doubt anxious to get home and out of the damp. "What is the way back to the main Apathy Road?"

"All roads will lead there if you follow them for long enough," he said vaguely. And then he politely excused himself and hurried on.

"Doesn't anyone around here give a straight answer?" demanded Timmy. "Hey you!" he called to a young man who was rushing by under an umbrella. "Can you tell us the way to Apathy Road?"

"Keep going straight ahead and you might reach Compromise," the young man called back. "You never know, they might tell you the way!"

"Honestly!" said Timmy. "What's wrong with the people around here?"

"I don't think they can give a straight answer," said Jack. "Most of the people at the Fair couldn't either. I think that's what happens when you're…well, wishy-washy and don't really know what to believe."

"That's what Mr Weighty would say," said Hezekiah.

Timmy scoffed at that notion. "Anyway," he said, "my stomach hurts and I'm starving hungry! Isn't there anything to eat around here?" It was true that Timmy looked a bit pasty. Despite all the food he had consumed, none of it seemed to have done him much lasting good.

"Look," said Jack, and pointed at a sign. It read: 'Compromise: the Town for Everybody'.

"That's not the way to the Weightys' stall," said Hezekiah. And now it was abundantly obvious that they had left the Fair altogether and were heading away in another direction entirely.

"Who cares about the Weightys' stall," said Timmy. "We'll see if we can get something to eat in Compromise!"

The mist grew even thicker, the rain continued to fall, and the dull daylight of late afternoon began to fade. There seemed nothing left to do but to keep walking somewhere even as the crowd around them thinned and vanished into the trees and the mist. All the other people were probably safe and dry at home. Jack and Hezekiah and Timmy were left alone in a land of marshland and trees.

And ahead, for good or ill, lay Compromise.

Somewhere they missed their turn to Compromise. There were no further encouraging signs or roads to show them where the town of Compromise might be. Even the road signs were not definite in this part of Err and, as they followed the narrow road onwards and the trees grew thicker around them, they knew that they were lost. Occasionally they saw someone or heard the voices of people going home. Timmy shouted out that they were lost and he had a loud voice that carried far and wide, but no one appeared to rescue them.

At last they saw a strange vehicle slowly approaching them. It had three wheels and seats like large armchairs facing front and back. It was slow but it had a roof to keep the rain off and looked sturdy and comfortable. Hezekiah said it was an Atob.

"That's a stupid name," said Timmy as they all watched it approach.

Hezekiah looked surprised.

"What does it mean?" asked Jack.

"Atob?" asked Hezekiah, clearly puzzled that they didn't understand. "Well, it means A to B of course. It takes you from A to B!"

They moved across to the edge of the road as the Atob came closer, hoping it would stop as they waved it down. Then through the mist and the gloom they saw the words 'Wander Palm: Prophetic Mystery Teller' painted boldly on the side.

"Hey!" Timmy leapt out and waved his arms wildly. "Hey! Remember me? Can you give me a ride? Stop! Please!"

Ms Wander Palm looked nothing like she had earlier. She was seated in one of the armchairs that faced backwards towards the three boys. She spoke to the driver and the Atob stopped, and the three boys moved closer, thankful for any help, even that of Wander Palm. That's when they realised that she looked normal and uninteresting in a faded skirt and knitted jumper.

She looked very tired too; and old; she had wrinkles that she didn't seem to have earlier; and most discouraging of all, she looked distinctly annoyed.

"It's the three pranksters, is it?" she said, and there was something quite nasty in the way she said it, as if she was glad that they were out there in the rain looking wet and miserable.

"Not me!" said Timmy. "It was them, not me! I paid you money…!"

Wander Palm looked at Timmy and then at Jack and Hezekiah, one by one, as if they were horrid little bugs that she might enjoy squashing under the wheels of her strange chariot.

"I've got more money to pay for a ride!" said Timmy, and he put his hand into his pocket and brought out his few remaining coins, holding them out to Wander Palm.

Wander Palm looked at them hesitatingly, and then, before she had the time to move, the coins unfurled delicate wings and, with the swiftness of the blink of an eye, they soared far out of reach up into the grey, misty sky.

Timmy stared stupidly at his empty hand. "But they were normal money," he said in an awestruck, horrified tone. Only Jack knew what Timmy meant: that the coins were from England, not from Err at all.

Wander Palm seemed unsurprised at the flight of the money and looked at Timmy with the greatest disdain. "This is what becomes of naughty boys," she said.

"Jack! You give her money!" demanded Timmy as Wander Palm prepared to go on her way.

Jack remembered the five pence piece that he still had in his pocket and he slowly removed it. He did not attempt to stop it from flying, despite Timmy's panicked remonstrations to hold it tightly. He looked at the small five pence which was unmoving in his hand, and it lay there without protest and without wings – until Wander Palm leant forward suddenly and plucked it from his hand, securing it quickly in her pocket.

"Can you take us to a town?" Timmy asked eagerly.

"To Aletheia?" asked Hezekiah.

"I have only accepted payment for your disgraceful behaviour," Wander Palm said with a horrible smile. "I would never give *you* a ride! You deserve all that is coming to you! You deserve the dire punishment that will come to you this night!" She gestured to her driver to move on, and, with Timmy proclaiming his innocence after her, the Atob moved slowly, steadily away and was at last swallowed up in the misty gloom ahead.

"This is all your fault!" said Timmy, furious with Jack and Hezekiah. "If you had never interfered and been so stupid with the Palm lady, we might have been rescued by now!"

"If you had never run away to start with...!" retorted Hezekiah.

"You interfering little brat...!" Timmy went to grab Hezekiah. "I didn't want you to come after me! I was doing very well on my own...!"

Hezekiah ducked away from Timmy. "Anyway," he shot back, "what do you think *Auntie Wander Palm* would do to help? She'd probably take you away to her witch's house and tell you lies about how great you're going to be…!"

"She didn't tell lies! How dare you… She's not a witch!"

"Well, she's certainly not an angel! Is she Jack? In fact, she's a thief! She even took Jack's money!"

Jack ignored the altercation. He was standing very still, looking around them into the grey shadows and darkness that was pressing closer. He was almost certain that he saw flickering, glittering eyes watching them where they stood by the deserted roadside. Jack thought of the Snares he had heard about and touched his head, thankful to feel the soothing helmet on his head that kept the worst of his fears away. He touched the Bible in the pouch at his side. And then he looked at Hezekiah. "Where is your Bible, Zek?" he asked.

Hezekiah stopped his ducking and diving and Timmy turned to stare at Jack.

"We're about to die of cold or starve to death in a foreign country and you want to know where his Bible is?" said Timmy. "You would think it's enough that I'm lost at night with you two, without you both going completely mad!"

"My Bible!" exclaimed Hezekiah in dismay. "Jack! We didn't put on all our armour when we left the Weightys' tent!"

Timmy groaned. "You're not still playing the game about war and armour, are you?" he sneered.

"I left behind my body armour and shield," Jack said in a subdued voice. "And my school rucksack too. I still haven't eaten my marmite sandwiches."

"Utterly mad!" said Timmy.

"I haven't got my helmet and Bible," Hezekiah said with a sort of strangled sob in his voice.

"Umm…Hellloooo!" said Timmy. "Is anybody thinking about food and perhaps somewhere warm and dry to spend the night? Let's get our priorities right here!"

But Jack looked into the shadows again and he knew what his priorities were.

They needed to escape the Snares.

They found a dry spot under a big tree with spreading branches which saved them from the dripping rain. As far as they could tell they were in a thick forest but at least it was some shelter from the unpleasant damp around them.

"It's dry here," said Jack, trying to be cheerful. "If we clear away these stones…"

"What are we going to eat?" demanded Timmy. He had lapsed into silence for the last while; he complained of tummy ache and Hezekiah, who generally did not have the knack of soothing Timmy, informed them it was because Timmy had eaten Wishy-Washy food.

"If you don't stop saying stupid things I'll gag you!" exclaimed Timmy.

"If you hadn't run away and eaten the wrong food…" retorted Hezekiah.

"Shhh…" hissed Jack.

There was sudden silence amongst them. Jack turned slowly and searched the forbidding forest behind them. He had heard a snigger; a horrible, nasty laugh of *something* that was out there. He wished he had a light, any light at all. But did he really want to see what it would reveal? Were they really at the mercy of cruel and shadowy Snares that might take them captive?

"What?" asked Timmy.

"What is it, Jack?" said Hezekiah.

"Nothing," muttered Jack. He sincerely hoped that he was right.

They all leant back against the big tree, staying close together.

"What was it Wander Palm said about '*punishment this night*'?" Hezekiah asked in a subdued, shaky voice. "Do you think she has powers to make things happen…?"

"No," said Jack. "We know she was just saying things. It's just the way she speaks."

For once Timmy didn't disagree. For once he hoped that Jack was right.

They were all sleepy now, Timmy in particular, and he was the first to fall asleep. Hezekiah murmured to himself and Jack thought he was praying; but then Hezekiah, too, fell asleep. Jack stayed awake a little longer. He thought one of them should keep watch: what for he still wasn't sure. But he knew that something was out there, watching and waiting, just beyond the poor evening light that was fading…fading away to night.

CHAPTER 12
TAKEN CAPTIVE!

It was dark when they awoke. Timmy opened his eyes and jerked upright in fright when he remembered that they were lost in a dark forest. That woke Jack and Hezekiah too. They stood and stretched their cramped limbs, their eyes gradually adjusting to the night darkness. They looked around them uneasily, hearing strange sounds in the trees.

"I don't like it here," said Timmy.

"Well, I don't think that any of us would have exactly chosen to be here," said Hezekiah, not particularly meaning to be sarcastic.

"We need to get help," said Timmy.

"I think we already know that," said Hezekiah, definitely being sarcastic this time.

Jack's tummy rumbled with hunger; it was way past dinnertime and all three of them were hungry, wet and chilled. But none of this was as concerning as the eerie glittering eyes of shadows that were watching them, that now appeared to be slowly approaching them through the trees.

"Did you see that?" Timmy suddenly took a step backwards and clutched Jack's arm in fright.

"They're watching us," said Jack. "I think they probably followed us from the Fair."

Hezekiah stood rigid and wild-eyed.

"What are they?" asked Timmy. "Shoo! Go away! We're armed! We've got…" he looked frantically around for something that might help. He grabbed a stick from the forest floor. "We've got weapons!"

Jack heard a snigger; a cold laugh. He knew that the shadowy things were Snares and that the Snares realised that he and Hezekiah and Timmy had nothing to fight them off with. Somehow he knew that sticks and stones would have no effect on them. After all, they were shadows.

Hezekiah's trembling hand touched his arm. "They're Snares, Jack," he said. "*Snares!*"

"What do we fight them with?" asked Jack. "What did they teach you at school?"

"I don't remember," said Hezekiah. "I don't remember!"

Jack tried frantically to think what to do. Of the three of them his mind seemed the most focused and it suddenly occurred to him that his helmet was helping him to stay calm and brave. His hand closed suddenly on the Bible that was encased securely in the pouch at his side. He pulled it out and held it firmly in his hand. It shone! It was like it said in the Bible: the Word of God was a lamp for footsteps and a light for the path ahead[8]. In Err it seemed that this came true literally.

"Zek!" he exclaimed. "Look! My Bible!"

"That's it!" said Hezekiah in sudden excitement. "The Bible is our weapon against them!"

There was a definite hesitation among the shadows that moved toward them.

And then one of the Snares spoke. "He's got a Bible!" it hissed angrily. "I thought you said they had no weapon!"

"They can speak!" Timmy said faintly.

"Not that boy!" said another Snare, "the other one. The other boy! He hasn't got anything and he's been encouraging us all day!"

"Not me!" exclaimed Hezekiah, his voice shrill with fear.

"Encouraging?" Timmy squeaked in fright. "Do they mean me? What are they talking about? What *are* they? I don't want them here! Make them go away, Jack! Show them that Bible again!"

Jack held his Bible high. It glowed strong and triumphant above them, shedding light that the Snares seemed to fear.

But they were still there beyond the light.

"Ignore that boy," commanded a big Snare. It towered above the other Snares. "Take the other boy! The other one is ours!"

"No!" shouted Hezekiah. "You can't take me! The Lord Jesus has set me free from you!"

"Not that boy!" the leader commanded above the confusion that Hezekiah's statement seemed to cause. "We can't take him, he doesn't belong to us, take the other one!"

"No!" Timmy shouted in terror. "I'm a Christian too! I've got a Bible somewhere at home! I'm nothing to do with you!"

There was a moment of awful, sickening sniggering amongst the shadows.

"We are the Snares of Pride and Self and Arrogance and Boasting and Love-of-Riches and False Teaching and many other things besides," a shadow hissed.

"You've been honouring us all day!" said another.

"You've been giving us a place in your life!"

"You refuse to turn to the cross," another taunted. "You have chosen your own way! You belong to us!"

"I haven't! I'm not! I'm not like that! Tell them, Jack!" Timmy's words were tripping over themselves in terrible fright.

"You don't have anything to fight us with!" a Snare mocked.

"He does!" said Timmy, trying to push Jack forward and hide behind him. "Tell them, Jack! You fight them! Fight them off with your Bible!"

"It's no good boy!" the big Snare leader hissed scornfully. "You cannot claim the protection of the Bible: you don't even believe it!"

The Snare's big, glittering eyes looked fleetingly uncertain as he glanced at Jack and Hezekiah. Jack was frantically trying to think what they ought to be doing to help Timmy. There must be something! The big Snare seemed to know that there was still something they could do to save Timmy!

"I've got a book too!" Timmy frantically rummaged in his rucksack and pulled out the book 'The Real Me: Learning to Love Yourself' that he had purchased at the Recycle Centre. But even as he looked at the book, Timmy was filled with sudden horror. This book about himself and how good he was would not defend him against these frightening creatures of the night. They didn't think he was good at all!

There was no restraining the horrible mirth of the watching Snares when they saw the book in Timmy's trembling hand.

"I helped to write that!" chortled one.

"There's not much in *that* that could scare us!" another boasted.

"That's nothing to do with the Bible!" said a third.

Many other Snares crowded through the trees and jostled around their companions, laughing at the terror stricken boy and the book that had dropped from his limp hand.

"Take him!" the Snare leader commanded.

Timmy shrieked in terror and hid behind Jack and Hezekiah, clutching at both of them wildly as if they might just save him.

Jack held the Bible high above them. The wonderful, comforting light of the Bible spilled around them. It was the only thing Jack could think of that might save Timmy from his fate. But the shadows of the sniggering Snares pressed closer and closer around them. The light from the Bible momentarily deterred the Snares from the capture of Timmy, but slowly and surely they circled closer and, notwithstanding the light they feared, the big Snare leader urged the Snare shadows forward to take poor Timmy away.

"Wait!" shrieked Timmy as a shadowy hand reached out and entwined around him. "Wait! I've got a DVD! I got it at the Recycle Centre!" and with his one free hand, the other still clutching wildly at Jack, he rummaged in his rucksack and drew out the '*You are the best*' DVD.

The laughter of the Snares was horrible to hear: the mocking, the taunts as the Snares realised that Timmy had nothing left with which to defend himself against those he had drawn to him through his rebellion and unbelief. He was without hope, and whilst the Snares hissed and shrank back and cackled in fear when Jack spilled the light of the Bible on them, there were too many to be long kept from their purpose.

They dragged Timmy away from the tree where they had slept and towards the darkness of the forest. He put up a good fight with his punches and his kicks and his loud shrieks of protest but the shadow creatures held him unrelenting in their grasps and his protests only amused them.

"Your Bible!" pleaded Timmy. "Let me have your Bible, Jack!"

Jack did not need Hezekiah's urgent pleading to keep the Bible; not for anything would he let go of that strong, unwavering source of light and strength and Timmy seemed to know it was impossible for Jack to part with the Bible.

"Wait!" shouted Jack. "Wait! Where are you taking him?"

"Where he belongs!" sniggered a Snare.

"Let's take him to False Teaching," suggested another, "he'll like it there!"

"You can meet our friend Ms Palm again!"

"Your pocket, Jack! What's in your pocket?" screamed Timmy. "Give them money to let me go!"

Jack felt in his pocket for something, *anything* to help Timmy who was slowly being taken further and further away into the darkness of the forest. He knew he had no money but curiously his fingers closed around the small, carved stick that old Reuben Duffle had given him in Aletheia. With sudden inspiration Jack threw the stick with all his might toward the Snares. To his astonishment it did not land short or float aimlessly through the air, but it flew like a rocket from his hand and...

BOOM!

There was a sudden explosion of white light and sparks and what even looked like fireworks. Snares fell away from Timmy in astonishment and terror and Hezekiah gave a sudden cry of excitement. Timmy yelled in triumph as he leapt free of their hold and made a dash for freedom. It seemed he would gain it too. For a moment the Snares were utterly dismayed.

"A prayer!" one hissed.

"Who's praying?" another asked fearfully.

"Are there more prayers coming?"

"We can't take him against that type of prayer!"

The Snare leader was re-gathering his troops and watching carefully as Timmy almost reached Jack and safety.

"Run!" shouted Timmy. "Run for your life!"

Shadows don't worry about boys that run. They merely glide after them. The glinting eyes of the Snare leader looked victorious.

"There are no more prayers," he hissed. "They wouldn't need to run if there were! Take him now!"

"No!" screamed Timmy. "Throw something else! Jack!"

"It was the stick!" gasped Jack. "The stick Mr Duffle gave me! They must be to do with him praying for us!"

Timmy looked aghast. "I threw my stick away!" he said in a piteous voice. "I didn't know they were special! How could I know? He was just a mad old man…!"

This time Timmy went quietly. The Snares closed quickly about him and grasped him in their shadowy hands, weaving their strange cobwebby bonds about him. There was no mercy in their eyes and there was no hope for Timmy. Timmy had thrown away the prayers of an old warrior; he had refused to acknowledge his need to be saved and set free from his sin; he had armed himself with a book and a DVD which had no power because they weren't the truth of the Bible; he had devoted himself to pride and self and false teaching and everything that was rude and arrogant and against the will of God. And so, the Snares of sin that bound people who gave themselves to all of those wretched, selfish things had come to take him away. Jack watched them go, clutching his Bible in his hand, frantic that they might take him or Hezekiah too. But they feared a Christian with the weapon of the Bible and they certainly feared the light that shone from the Word of God.

Hezekiah who had stood silent and trembling and horribly frightened at the whole scene roused himself after the success of the prayer-stick. He called encouragement to Timmy even as

Timmy vanished entirely into the darkness of the forest.

"You must pray, Barmy!" he shouted urgently. "Ask God to help you and set you free! Then we can come and rescue you! Remember to PRAY!"

It wasn't clear if Timmy heard Hezekiah's urgent pleas.

He vanished completely from their sight and at last Hezekiah fell silent.

The two boys were left alone.

CHAPTER 13
THE RESCUE CRAFT

It was dark and still under the trees of the forest. Jack used his Bible as a light to show them the way and he and Hezekiah together retraced their steps to the small clearing where they had slept, crunching over dried leaves and small twigs and branches, back to the big tree. But there was little to linger for there.

"Shall we try to find our way out of here? We must find help for Timmy." Hezekiah was still trembling and Jack now realised that there was something he had that could help.

He reluctantly removed his helmet from his head and handed it to Hezekiah. "Here," he said, "we'll share it and take it in turns as we go along. We'll take it in turns with the Bible too. You go first."

Hezekiah quickly fitted the helmet to his head and took hold of the light that was the Bible. "Oh!" he said. And then, "oh!" again. He didn't really need to explain what he was feeling: Jack saw the relief and gladness in the expression on his face.

Jack himself felt bereft of support and encouragement without his helmet and Bible but he tried as best as he could to keep his mind focussed on the things that the helmet helped with. The helmet helped you to remember that, because you were saved and had trusted in the Lord Jesus, you were set free from sin. The Lord Jesus was victorious over all the enemies and problems a Christian might face, and so you could be strong and brave because the Lord Jesus had already defeated foes like Snares; He enabled Christians to defeat the wicked things that were around them and He had also sent another Helper[9] to help Christians win the battles around them. There was no need to be afraid! But it was easy to forget that when the Snares gathered around.

Jack wondered what the time was. How long had it been since they had left the Fair? How long since they had got lost in the forest? Were people looking for them yet? He put his hand in his pocket and it closed around his spy watch. It was a sudden, strange fancy, but he wondered if his spy watch, which told the time in lots of different countries, happened to know the time in the land of Err. He flicked it open and checked the dial. Amazingly his watch now showed 'True Aletheia Time'! It was 10.54pm, and underneath the time it also said '*Time for bed!*' So much time had passed! No wonder he was so tired and hungry! Hezekiah was tired and hungry too but neither boy complained. They just trudged on, walking steadily through the forest, following the light of the Bible. They both agreed that walking uphill, in the opposite direction Timmy had taken, seemed the best way. They picked their way carefully through the trees, around patches of boggy ground, past thorn bushes and shrubs, following the light of the Bible. They found a faint path and followed it onwards. Once they saw a sign on a post by the path. *'Alternative Teaching this way'* it read. It pointed back the way they had come and they knew that they were right to be going away from a place called Alternative Teaching.

They didn't talk much about how far they were walking and how many creatures of the night they saw in the darkness. At last the trees began to thin and the mist seemed less intense, and suddenly Hezekiah stopped and pointed. "Look, Jack!" he said.

And when Jack looked upwards he saw the cross of the city of Aletheia, high on a hill, illuminated against the dark of the night sky.

And then they knew that they were no longer lost: for now they could follow the cross.

It did not take the boys long to realise that they would not make it back to Aletheia that night. They could still see the cross, they knew the direction that they should take and they even found a faint path to follow. But they were too tired to keep walking all the way back up Apathy Road to the safety of Aletheia. They were not really afraid. The fear receded when either Jack or Hezekiah put the helmet on and held the Bible in their hand. And there was the additional comfort of the cross high on the hill. But nevertheless they must, they decided, find somewhere to lie down and sleep for at least some of the night.

They were quietly discussing this and testing the ground beneath a big, sheltering pine tree when they heard a strange sound. It wasn't exactly an engine, not like the ones that Jack knew at home anyway, but it was something that didn't sound like a human or an animal, and it was definitely coming their way. They both withdrew to the tree, standing back in the shadows and peeping out to watch what might be coming down the path towards them.

And then, through the stillness of the night, they heard a most welcome sound.

"I think I should drive now, Hugo! You almost hit that tree!"

"Henry!" breathed Hezekiah. Then, "It's Henry!" he shouted. "It's Henry, Jack!"

The conversation between Hugo and Henrietta Wallop continued:

"I wouldn't have swerved if you hadn't grabbed the wheel!"

"Are we still going the right way? Are you sure? Let's check the signal again!"

"We checked it a few minutes ago!"

"I know, but this path is so faint…"

"Stop grabbing the wheel, Henry!"

And that was when the twins noticed the two boys running down the path towards them.

Henrietta's shriek could have scared the creatures of Err for miles around. "We've found them! Oh, Hugo, we've found them!" And the next moment Henrietta was racing down the path towards Jack and Hezekiah, flinging her arms around them both in overwhelming relief.

There were a few moments of chaos when everyone talked over the top of everyone else and nobody was bothered about much except enjoying the wonderful feeling of being found and

rescued and reunited once more. Then Hugo and Henrietta put the two tired boys in the incredible contraption in which they had travelled to meet them. Hezekiah was particularly excited with their transport.

"It's Mr Weighty's own Rescue Craft!" he exclaimed in excitement.

Jack had seen the big white letters on the side of the strange machine: 'WEIGHTY'S RESCUE CRAFT' and he had never seen anything like it. It was a mix of the oldest, oddest tractor, and something like a very big quad bike. It had four big wheels, big armchair-type seats facing forward and a big settee-type seat facing backwards. There were various cupboards and storage areas between the front and back of the Craft and a very large steering wheel in the front.

"It belongs to Mr Weighty," Henrietta explained to Jack.

"I think that's probably the obvious bit, Henry," said Hugo.

"Mr Weighty's Craft is one of the best!" said Hezekiah. "I've always wanted to see it!"

"I think Mr Weighty sort-of added lots of things," said Henrietta. "And Mrs Weighty probably added the cushions and sleeping bags and blankets that we found."

"It's got the Rescuer's Kit and Mission Detector and everything else we need on board," said Hugo. "That's how we found you!"

"Oh," said Jack, trying to take in the explanation, particularly of how they had been found. He remembered Mr Weighty mentioning a 'Mission Detector' when he explained how people communicated in the land of Err.

"Look," said Hugo pointing at a strange screen by the steering wheel. "You can see from this Mission Detector that we've been searching for you …" and he pointed to the top of the screen, which showed *Hezekiah Amos Wallop* and *Jack Arnold Merryweather* in white, scrawled writing. "Well, the map on the screen can locate Christians in need, Christians who are lost, anybody who is praying for help, you know, things like that."

Jack and Hezekiah both leaned forward from the back settee where they were sitting and stared at the white dot on the enlarged map of Err which showed where they had been found. The closer you peered at the screen the larger the image became, until you could almost see the tall pine tree under which they had considered sleeping that night.

"I'm glad you came," said Hezekiah.

"Oh, Zek," said Henrietta, "as if we would have left you alone in Err all night! We had to come!"

"Yes, we did," Hugo said more wryly and Jack caught a glance between the twins that he did not understand.

The boys removed their armour boots, got into cosy sleeping bags, and curled up on the big settee at the back of the Rescue Craft. Hugo started up the Craft and it began to trundle down the narrow path once more, first slowly and then with increasing speed.

"What about Timmy?" asked Jack, as Henrietta unpacked a picnic and passed them cheese sandwiches and cups of hot tomato soup.

"You'd better eat up before you both fall asleep," she said, watching them both with touching anxiety.

"Barmy was taken by Snares," said Hezekiah, and he shuddered slightly in the darkness.

"We know, Zek," said Henrietta.

"How do you know?" asked Jack.

"We know because of this," said Hugo. He changed the name at the top of the Mission Detector screen in the Rescue Craft to 'Timothy Trial'. "It took us a while to get it to work," he admitted, "we kept putting in the name Barmy Bats. We couldn't remember

Barmy's real name at all!"

Beside Timmy's name at the top of the screen were the words *'Taken by Snares; likely direction False Teaching'*. Jack thought that the Detector was a bit like Sat Nav except that it gave different information. But Jack didn't try to explain that. Hugo and Henrietta and Hezekiah would likely never have heard of Sat Nav and Jack didn't think he would be able to explain.

"We can't see where Timmy is yet," said Henrietta. "But we'll get it working properly soon."

"I've been thinking, and I might know why it doesn't show all the details yet," said Hugo.

"Why?" asked Henrietta.

"I remember Harold explaining about the importance of people praying," said Hugo. "Timmy has to pray for help and then we get more information about where to find him."

"I told him to pray!" Hezekiah piped up. "Maybe he will pray!"

"You know something, Hugo," said Henrietta, "I think you might actually be right!"

"Don't sound too surprised!" said Hugo.

"Well, it *is* the first time, after all," retorted Henrietta.

Hezekiah smiled sleepily and snuggled down in his sleeping

bag. As far as he was concerned his troubles were over. They had been rescued; the rest was up to the twins.

Jack stayed awake a little longer than Hezekiah. There was something alluring about bouncing along in this strange, settee-bed at the back of the Rescue Craft. Through the mist he could see stars in the sky, and the trees that still loomed large by the side of the narrow road no longer looked forbidding. The shadows had passed; perhaps the danger had passed too.

It transpired, as the Rescue Craft bounced and bumbled its way down the road, that the presence of Hugo and Henrietta in the wilds of Err was less 'official' than might have been supposed. When Hugo and Henrietta realised that Jack and Hezekiah had disappeared, and when they hadn't reappeared by the close of the Wishy-Washy Fair, it was decided that someone should go and find them. A few other factors appeared to conspire to ensure that it was Hugo and Henrietta alone who set out on this task. First, their brother Harold, who was to come for them all, was delayed.

"He had to go on an emergency rescue to Broken," explained Hugo.

"So it was down to us to come and get you!" said Henrietta.

She was quite cheerful about the turn of events, especially since they had found Jack and Hezekiah.

"Well," Hugo said more hesitantly and truthfully, "Mr Weighty was going to come…"

"But he was going to wait until the morning!"

"Mr Weighty wanted to leave early in the morning," said Hugo, "as soon as he had more information, he said."

"But we thought we shouldn't wait," said Henrietta. "We couldn't just go home and leave you two alone out here somewhere! So…well, here we are!"

They certainly were. Jack didn't ask how they had acquired Mr Weighty's own Rescue Craft or whether Mr Weighty knew that it was now absent from his shed. Henrietta merely mentioned that it was "borrowed" and since Jack's eyes were closing in sleep, he asked no more.

CHAPTER 14
THE EXPLODING DRINK

It was light when Jack opened his eyes. The jolting had stopped and the strange *putt-putt* of the Rescue Craft engine had ceased. Beside him Hezekiah still slept peacefully and Henrietta was also asleep, curled up on the front seat in a sleeping bag. Hugo was close by picking handfuls of grass and twigs and leaves. It was morning and the sign up ahead read *'Welcome to Alternative Teaching: Keep an Open Mind!'*

"I thought we'd stop and refuel," explained Hugo.

"With grass?" asked Jack.

Hugo stuffed handfuls of the grass and twigs he had collected into a small hole at the side of the Rescue Craft. "I think it takes just about anything," he said. "Mr Weighty really is a very clever inventor! He's changed things so that it'll go just about anywhere and run on just about anything. I'd love to make something like this!"

Jack thought he would too. Imagine having a tractor that would run on grass and leaves and old sticks and twigs and go anywhere! He wished that Grandad was there to see it.

"Umm…where are we exactly?" he asked as he wriggled free of his sleeping bag, trying not to disturb Hezekiah.

Hugo gestured to the sign. "Alternative Teaching," he said.

That wasn't exactly what Jack meant. Really he meant to ask why on earth they were still in the middle of Err, and why they weren't safely at the Weightys' house, or even back in Aletheia by now.

"I thought we were going back to Aletheia," remarked Jack. It wasn't that he was disappointed as much as he was puzzled.

"Oh," said Hugo with dawning understanding, "didn't we explain last night? We're going to keep going and rescue Barmy."

Jack decided not to comment on that. There wasn't much he could do about it one way or another and he was secretly pleased that the adventure wasn't over and that they were going to help Timmy. The morning light had driven away the fears of the night and he definitely liked travelling in Mr Weighty's Rescue Craft.

"We can have breakfast here," said Hugo, "when Henry decides to wake up."

"I am awake!" Henrietta sat up suddenly and rubbed her eyes. "I probably wouldn't have fallen asleep at all if you'd let me drive!"

"Well, I would hope not!" retorted Hugo. "Or we would all have been in a ditch. But anyway," he winked at Jack, "I think boys should do all the driving, don't you Jack?"

There wasn't a safe answer to that, but Henrietta merely yawned and stretched and pulled herself out of her sleeping bag. "You're only saying that to annoy me," she said. "So I *won't* be annoyed!"

"Does that mean that I get to drive too?" Hezekiah's sleepy head appeared and he looked around him with interest. "Where are we?" he asked.

Hezekiah wasn't bothered that their current location was the small town of Alternative Teaching and that they were even further away from Aletheia than they had been the night before. He had unlimited faith in his two siblings' decisions, and besides, like Jack, he was pleased that their adventure would continue.

Jack got down from the Rescue Craft and wandered further down the road they were parked beside. Around the next corner were the houses and shops and paved streets of Alternative Teaching.

It was hard to say exactly what was odd about Alternative Teaching. There were small things, subtle differences, just a little here and there that was slightly different to the normal, solid homes that Jack knew and that were in Aletheia. It was a nice place, even a pretty place, and neat and tidy too. But there was a cottage with a triangular window in the wrong place, and a house with a round door, and a chimney poking out of a wall, and other odd little bits and pieces peering from the homes.

"They encourage alternative things here," remarked Hugo, joining Jack.

"It looks almost normal," said Jack.

"But it's not quite right, is it?" said Hugo.

There was a little café by the side of the road in Alternative Teaching and it was open and serving breakfast. There was some debate between Hugo and Henrietta whether it was safe to venture into the café for breakfast, but they had very little choice if they were to eat. Already their stores of food were badly depleted and at last they decided that if they sat at an outdoor table and only ate plain food, they would probably be alright.

"We'll put on our armour as well," said Hugo. "Then we'll really be okay."

They had enough armour between them, including the spare supplies of armour from Mr Weighty's Rescue Craft, to all be fully equipped and they approached the small café without concern. Everything felt different during the day. The sun was peeping through the trees that surrounded the small town and birds chirped cheerfully. Gone was the cold and fear of the night. It was just like a dream in the light of the morning sunshine. There was no longer any need to be afraid. In fact, they hardly seemed to need armour at all.

There was the lone figure of a man already seated at an outdoor table of the café and it was only when they reached him that Jack realised with surprise that it was Mr Wonky Dollar. He was wearing a new coat with a big red, silk hanky sticking out of the top pocket. He was drinking from a tall glass that contained strange, dark liquid that bubbled and fizzed as he swirled it around.

"Hello," said Jack.

Mr Dollar stared at him. "Oh!" he exclaimed. "It's you, is it? The boy who was kind enough to give me his very interesting Treasure Lego! Join me, dear boy! Yes, your friends too! Anyone who is a friend of this boy is a friend of mine! Sit, sit here, and... Dough!" he yelled, "a drink for my friends! Yes, yes, of course you must have a drink! I'm making big money from the Treasure

Lego which I must tell you about! Dough! DOUGH!"

At last a man appeared through the door of the café which was more of a dirty shack than a nice place to eat. 'Dough' was a very good name for the man. He was pasty and round and looked like a dough-ball. He waddled very slowly and contemplatively towards them. "I'm not deaf!" he protested. "What's the hurry? There is no hurry around here!"

He was right. The street was empty. Most folk were still asleep.

"Drinks for my friends here!" insisted Mr Dollar. "And some fresh bread for breakfast too! We're celebrating a most curious Treasure Lego find, such as Err has never seen before!"

Dough moved slowly off into the interior of the shack muttering something that didn't sound very complimentary. The café-shack didn't look very clean inside, and none of them wanted to drink that strange, bubbling dark liquid that Mr Dollar had, or eat the type of bread that a man like Dough was likely to make. And aside from that, was it safe? They had all been warned about eating and drinking the wrong things in Err.

Hugo and Henrietta exchanged glances.

Jack and Hezekiah watched them anxiously.

Now what should they do?

None of the three Wallops present had met Mr Wonky Dollar before but they had seen him now and again in parts of Aletheia and knew enough about him to be curious. He was notorious and they had heard tales of his love of money and his inability to keep it. So it was surprising to learn of his recent good fortune.

"Well," said Mr Dollar, settling back in the rickety seat outside the café. "That Treasure Lego really did bring me luck you know. I thought it might, I really did; first time I saw it. Red, I said to myself, red treasure will bring me luck!"

That didn't make much sense at all, to Jack at least. But Mr Dollar was firmly convinced of the worth of a red piece of lego. Hugo, Henrietta and Hezekiah had never seen lego and were most interested in Mr Dollar's account.

"One thousand Erona coins!" Mr Dollar leaned closer to them, apparently not wanting Mr Dough to hear this spectacular detail. "They're going to pay me one thousand Eronas for the Treasure Lego!"

Jack stared at him. "Are you sure?" he asked, quite certain Mr Dollar was either wildly exaggerating or badly mistaken.

Wonky Dollar nodded. "I had my fortune told at Wishy-Washy Fair," he confided. "The mystery lady told me I might make money from the Treasure Lego and that I should have it examined at the Academy of Science-Explains-All. And she was right!"

"Was the mystery lady called Wander Palm?" asked Hezekiah.

"Yes, yes!" agreed Mr Dollar. "That's her. Lovely lady! I'm going to give her a share of my new fortune too!"

Hezekiah and Jack exchanged incredulous glances. They would not have described Ms Wander Palm as a '*lovely lady*'.

Mr Dough returned and placed a big jug of the strange dark, sparkling liquid and four glasses on the table. Then he added a fresh loaf of bread, butter, jam, and five plates and knives. Mr Dollar fumbled in his pockets, clanking his treasure boxes and reluctantly removing a handful of coins to pay Mr Dough. Then he carefully shoved the treasure boxes deep into his pockets again. "I got an advance on the one thousand Eronas I'm owed," he said. "Some of the coins already flew away, but I won't lose them again!"

"But who bought the piece of lego?" asked Jack, still feeling bewildered.

"The Academy of Science-Explains-All!" said Mr Dollar. His face took on a cunning expression. "I had a feeling it was an unusual find, *very* unusual! And the mystery lady helped me see I should take it to the Academy who immediately realised its worth and bought it from me!"

"I've heard of the Academy," said Hugo. "They don't believe in the Bible there."

"I don't know about that," said Mr Dollar, "but they're very clever people!"

"And what will the Academy do with it?" asked Jack.

"They're going to analyse it!" said Mr Dollar. "Do you know that the Treasure Lego is likely to be millions of years old? Why, they think it probably belonged to a pre-historic civilisation!"

"I don't think so," said Henrietta. "God made the world[10]. There's nothing in the world that's millions of years old!"

"Really I should have charged more for it," said Mr Dollar. He was contemplating the worth of the 'Treasure Lego' whilst Jack tried to understand how on earth such a silly mistake could have occurred.

"I don't think the lego is millions of years old," he said.

"Definitely not," agreed Hugo.

"My dear boy," said Mr Dollar, "you have no idea! The Academy has some very clever scientists! They know all about these things! What would you know compared to them?"

He had a good point of course, and Hugo fervently wished he'd paid more attention to the Creation teacher at school, or that he could call on Mr and Mrs Markerpen, the Outpost Rescuers who worked in the towns around the Academy of Science-Explains-All. He needed to know so much more before he could hope to help a man like Mr Dollar who was naturally going to believe the scientists and even this mystery teller woman rather than children.

"It was made in a factory somewhere," said Jack. "Maybe it was made in England or China or somewhere, but it was probably only made a few years ago!"

Hezekiah giggled inadvertently and then put his hand over his mouth.

Mr Dollar shook his head indulgently. Nothing seemed to dampen his spirits. "You kids should leave it to the experts," he advised.

"God is the expert!" said Henrietta.

Mr Dollar took no notice of Henrietta.

"But now," he said, and he leaned expectantly towards Jack. "What I'm thinking is this. We could go into business together, you and me. You bring in Treasure Lego to Err, and I'll sell it to the Academy for millions of Eronas!"

Jack shook his head, thinking how crazy the whole conversation was. In any case, surely the scientists would find out at any moment that the piece of lego had 'Made in China' or 'Made in England' printed on the back! Perhaps Jack should bring the lego box back to Err to show them their mistake.

"I don't think it would work," said Jack, wanting to let Mr Dollar down gently.

"The whole idea is absolutely rotten bananas!" said Henrietta bluntly.

Hugo kicked her under the table.

"Ow!" she exclaimed. "What did you do that for?"

"Millions of Eronas to be made," said Mr Dollar, taking no notice of the altercation between the twins. "Now, you must all eat up!" encouraged Mr Dollar, focussing mainly on Jack. He still thought that he could persuade him to cooperate with his business schemes. He poured the dark liquid into the glasses and cut up the bread, distributing it around the table.

Hugo was eyeing the strange drink as if he would like to tip it away without Mr Dollar observing.

"Come on now," said Mr Dollar, "I've paid good money for this!"

Jack politely but reluctantly picked up the glass and took a sip. Hugo did the same, inadvertently taking a big gulp of the drink. They felt sorry for Mr Dollar, and after all, he was only trying to be kind. Hezekiah looked wide-eyed and, when Mr Dollar wasn't looking, he managed to tip some of his drink onto the ground. His eyes widened even more when the grass the drink landed on sizzled and hissed and began shrivelling and turning brown. Very anxiously Hezekiah watched Jack and Hugo's reaction to what they had swallowed.

The drink was sour and sickly and flavoured with something earwigs might taste of. Perhaps Mr Dough had put earwigs into his drinks in the untidy shack. The drink made Hugo and Jack feel peculiar in their heads and their helmets suddenly felt too tight. Worse still, Jack was certain he saw shadows stealing from behind the big tree close by and edging towards them. Had the Snares come back again…?

"What else do you have in your pockets just now, my boy?" asked Mr Dollar. "Show me again! There might be something else we could use to make more money! There's no point in waiting until you can bring lots of Treasure Lego back to Err! We need to seize opportunities now!"

Jack slowly removed the contents of both of his pockets. He felt hot and slow and sleepy. On the table he placed his spy watch and the only other thing he had left: Mr Duffle's other carved stick, the one that Timmy had thrown away and Jack had picked up. Jack stared at the small stick. He had forgotten all about it. He could have used it to help Timmy fight the Snares last night!

Mr Dollar picked up Mr Duffle's stick and quickly threw it straight back onto the table with an astonished exclamation. "It burnt me!" he said. "Whatever is it?"

Henrietta leaned forward, equally astonished. Yes, there really was an angry red mark on Mr Dollar's hand where he had picked up the stick.

Jack felt befuddled and strange and Hugo looked as if he was crossing his eyes and falling asleep. Henrietta, who had not had any of the dangerous drink, gave Hugo a sharp kick under the table.

"Wake up!" she hissed at him.

Hugo sat up sharply and glared at his sister. "I feel weird," he said. "I'm just tired!" But then he looked more closely at the small stick that had burned Mr Dollar's hand. "I've seen something like that before," he said. "I wonder…"

"I wonder…" Mr Dollar said too, staring at the stick and looking most intrigued. "I wonder if they would buy this down at Drink-n-Drugs-Upon-Hollow. They like strange concoctions down there…I wonder…"

Jack picked up the stick. It felt perfectly normal. "I don't think they'll like this down there," he said, certain about that.

"You might be right," said Mr Dollar. "After all it burns! You're very brave to carry that around with you!"

Jack looked at the stick in his hand. It didn't burn him; it felt just right there.

And then Hezekiah reached forward and took the stick from Jack, and, as if he knew perfectly well what he was doing, he calmly dropped the stick into the jug of sparkling, dark liquid which he felt sure was full of danger.

WHOOSH!

There was a sudden explosion as some of the drink shot straight into the air!

"Flying Hens!" Mr Dollar exclaimed in astonishment. "Perfumed Pigs!"

They all watched as the drink bubbled and fizzed and wildly protested at the presence of the stick, and at last subsided into clear, harmless water. And just as strangely, the liquid in their glasses changed to harmless water too. Jack wondered if he only imagined it or if he really did hear the Snare shadows he had seen creeping towards them hissing softly in fear and disappointment.

"Dancing Cows!" said Mr Dollar. "I've never seen anything like it! Give me the stick! They'll pay good money for this at the Academy!"

But the small stick was completely gone. It had melted into the dark liquid and Jack took a sip of harmless water from his glass. It wasn't pure Water of Sound Doctrine, but he knew perfectly well it could no longer do him or anyone else any harm.

Mr Dollar looked disappointed when nothing spectacular happened to Jack when he drank the water. He had wondered whether Jack might grow wings or turn green and he would have none of it himself. "Where did you get the stick?" he urged. "Tell me about the stick!"

"A man in Aletheia gave it to me," said Jack. "He's called Mr Duffle and lives at Run-the-Race Retirement Complex."

"Is he a magician?" asked Mr Dollar.

"No," said Jack, "he prays. I think he prays a lot, and I think he prays when he carves sticks. That's why things happen with his sticks."

"Just as I thought!" exclaimed Hugo. "There are sticks like that in the Rescuer's Kit in the Rescue Craft. They come from people who are praying and represent the power of prayer! You are clever to think of dropping it in the drink, Zek!"

Hezekiah coloured with pleasure; secretly he was as surprised as any of them at the spectacular reaction of the stick.

Mr Dollar only looked puzzled at Hugo's explanation. "Prayer?" he echoed doubtfully. "I've heard people pray before but it's never been anything like that!"

They didn't really know how to explain the invisible power of prayer to Mr Dollar, and at last they left him at the table of the wayside café and prepared to return to the Rescue Craft.

"I still wish you had another piece of that Treasure Lego,"

said Mr Dollar as they parted.

The four travellers walked very thoughtfully through the quiet town of Alternative Teaching and back to the Craft. They felt defeated, as if they hadn't made the right impression on Wonky Dollar at all; they hadn't really been able to help him understand anything.

"You know," said Henrietta as they all climbed aboard the Craft once more, "there's definitely more to rescuing people than I ever thought there would be!"

"We don't have all the answers we need to help people," admitted Hugo.

"I think we need to know the Bible better," said Hezekiah.

"We need to learn to pray like Mr Duffle," said Jack.

He knew that Mr Duffle would know how to help a man like Mr Dollar. Mr Duffle, confined to the Run-the-Race Rest Home as he was, was still helping to rescue people in Err. And in the end it was Mr Duffle's prayers that had left the lasting impression on poor Wonky Dollar.

CHAPTER 15
DANGER! SNARES!

Mr Weighty's Rescue Craft seemed perfectly content to run on the grass and leaves and twigs that Hugo had stuffed inside its 'fuel' tank. It went smoothly onwards through the large, lush forest that led from Alternative Teaching all the way to Hollow Spring, continuing to the tall, dark, disorientating forest of False Teaching.

Jack was allowed a turn at driving the Rescue Craft and he felt that there was nothing equal to it in his life so far. Being sat by his Grandad and steering a giant combine harvester was one thing, but being completely in control of this fantastic and inexplicably strange mode of transportation was quite another. He was determined, even if it took him the rest of his life, that he would one day invent something like Mr Weighty's Rescue Craft. Hezekiah was allowed to drive too for a short while, but he struggled to reach all the pedals and reluctantly handed control back to Jack who was thrilled to be officially recognised as the second most important driver on their expedition. Henrietta protested loudly at not being given a chance to drive so Hugo gave her the job of navigation and exploring the on-board 'Mission Detector' system.

Henrietta removed the Mission Detector screen from beside the steering wheel and sat at the back on the settee with Hezekiah, quite content with her task. "Hey, this is really amazing, guys," she said. "It tells you far more than you would ever imagine! In fact, we really should have followed its instructions when we were at Alternative Teaching!"

"Great," said Hugo. "I can just hear the lectures we're going to get about how we weren't prepared for this rescue mission and didn't follow the instructions!" He was well aware that they were currently supposed to be listening to the Sunday preaching that took place every week by the cross in Aletheia. He wondered if he would ever dare to go back and face his father and mother again.

"It'll all be okay when we find Timmy and prove we've done the right thing," said Henrietta. But she too secretly wondered how long the search would go on. And she had never contemplated going missing for another whole day with a borrowed Rescue Craft that they had never got proper permission to use.

Jack and Hezekiah just went with the flow. There wasn't any

point in worrying about what they were missing when Jack in particular had not the faintest idea how to get back to his real home again. And anyway, in the meantime there was the wonder of riding in and driving the Rescue Craft, with the roof off, in the bright sunshine, the breeze rushing past them and keeping them nice and cool.

"You see," Henrietta explained her latest finding on the Detector, "it has buttons for weather, plants, ground conditions, animals and food and all sorts of other things too for every place in Err. So if we had looked up Alternative Teaching Food, like this…" she swivelled the screen around so that the boys in the front seat could read it. "You see?" she said. "It tells you all about the local drinks and warns…"

"*As with many other things in this area of Err,*" Hugo read from the screen, "*the drinks in Alternative Teaching are likely to muddle your mind and cloud your judgement. The local speciality, Black Beetle Beverage…*yuk! That's what we drank, Jack!" Hugo exclaimed, and Henrietta giggled. Then Hugo continued reading, "*Black Beetle Beverage is amongst the strongest mind muddler of them all. It is designed to open your mind to new possibilities, particularly those that are subtly against the teaching of the Bible. Rescuers should never imbibe Black Beetle Beverage and should* *immediately drink liberally of the Water of Sound Doctrine if they are ever tricked into doing so."*

"Well!" said Henrietta. "What do you think of that?"

"I suppose that when they wrote that they didn't know about Zek's trick with Mr Duffle's prayer stick that changed the drink," remarked Jack.

Hugo laughed. "You're right!" he said. "We should let them know! You might become famous for inventing that, Zek! What does it say about the town of False Teaching, Henry?"

Henrietta pressed buttons on the screen. "False Teaching... here we are...oh, boy!"

"What?" asked Hugo.

"Accessed through a dark, disorientating forest, False Teaching is notoriously difficult for Rescuers and other Christians to find if they do not have a mind open to exploring its possibilities." Henrietta paused in her reading and they all looked ahead to the outline of a dense forest that was some distance before them.

"False Teaching is thickly inhabited by Snares, and highly misleading. Nothing is reliable here, and even the sign posts have been known to trick those who do not enter False Teaching as a friend with an open mind." Henrietta paused again.

"Does that mean we actually have to go there with an open mind and not stick by what the Bible says?" asked Hezekiah, aghast.

"No, Zek!" said Henrietta. "At least, I don't think so! I think it means that if we go in our armour of God to rescue Timmy and take him away from False Teaching, then the place itself makes it as hard as possible for us to rescue Timmy! It doesn't want us there, you see?"

"Not exactly," said Hugo. "But we'll have to wait and see, won't we?"

The road they travelled, which was smoother than the bumpy track of the night before, appeared to be the long way round to False Teaching which was Timmy's last known likely destination. They could still see the trees of a thick forest ahead which they thought might be the massive fir trees that surrounded False Teaching, but the road twisted and turned and they seemed to make little progress for all the miles that they travelled. Of course, it helped to have the amazing Mission Detector which showed them the way, but it was sometime before Henrietta, the Detector expert, realised why the road they travelled was such a long way.

"I can see it now!" she said. "We had the Route-Finder showing all routes *via Hollow Spring*! We're going the long way round!

Jack didn't mind that much. He was still the driver and enjoyed driving down the smooth road, watching people pass, enjoying the strange sights and sounds of rural Err that weren't anything like those he would see at home. It felt safe in the Rescue Craft too. Not like it did when they were walking through the night.

"Is there any safe food at Hollow Spring?" asked Hugo. He was thinking of the severely depleted supplies of Mrs Weighty's food. Last night they had munched through sandwiches whenever they were hungry, had definitely finished all the chocolate muffins, and had eaten most of the biscuits. Now there was only the fruit left and there was hardly enough of that to even have a snack. They had not thought to save any food for another day. They had expected to be home by now.

Henrietta looked up Hollow Spring on the Mission Detector. "There's not likely to be any safe food exactly," she said slowly, reading what the screen had to say. "*The main danger of Hollow Spring is the trick it plays of making you feel fleetingly satisfied, but never really content,*" she read. "*You must trust nothing here.*"

"What exactly does that mean?" demanded Hugo.

"*The closer you get to False Teaching, the less you can trust the food and drink,*" continued Henrietta, "*including the area around Hollow Spring. Food here will generally be hollow or contain only tepid water and nothing of substance. For example, carrots may appear big and healthy, but they will only be a shell that quickly breaks apart and contains nothing…* Well, I don't like carrots so I wouldn't mind that!" Henrietta interjected into her reading, and then went on, "*You must beware of anything that appears substantial: nothing is quite what it seems.*"

"Great!" muttered Hugo. "I don't have a clue what that means but whatever it does mean it sounds as if we'll go hungry on top of everything else!"

"Well, don't blame me!" Henrietta flared up. "I didn't eat the last two chocolate muffins! Now we have none at all!"

"Whose idea was this whole trip anyway?" returned Hugo. "Who insisted we shouldn't wait for Mr Weighty?"

"Wait for Weighty!" Hezekiah said with a sudden giggle, but he lapsed into silence when he glanced at the twins; they did not see the joke.

"I suppose we should have let Mr Weighty take care of

everything in the morning, should we?" demanded Henrietta.

"I always said that!" yelled Hugo. "I was the one that always said…"

"I wasn't asking a question!" retorted Henrietta. "I was being sarcastic!"

"Well, your sarcasm…!"

"Umm…" Jack cleared his throat and suddenly slowed the Rescue Craft, pulling it to a stop at the side of the road. Jack pointed at the Detector screen on Henrietta's lap that was suddenly flashing red in the most alarming manner. They all peered at the screen and a sickening silence fell amongst them. In big bold, white letters was written:

"DANGER! SNARES!"

"Drive!" yelled Henrietta.

Jack pushed his foot down on the accelerator but nothing happened. Worse still, the reassuring putt-putt sound of the Rescue Craft engine faded and died away entirely.

Now Jack could see the Snares just ahead. In the daylight they were thick grey and black shadows, like the dark thunder clouds of a summer storm. And that's where they seemed to come from, falling out of a sky that was no longer full of sunshine, but was threatening to unleash the most ferocious thunder and rain.

"Henry!" said Hezekiah, clutching his sister, "what shall we do?"

Henrietta was white faced and almost speechless. "I don't know, Zek," she said.

"Everyone put on your armour," said Hugo. His voice was trembling but he was thinking hard. "And make sure you have your Bible in your hand."

"That's what they didn't like yesterday," said Jack, trying to keep his own voice steady. "They didn't like the Bible!"

It was hard with the fear of Snares upon them to calmly fasten on their armour and await their enemies. Cold seemed to penetrate them as the clouds grew thicker around them, and there were strange stirrings in the trees.

"We must collect fuel for the Craft," said Jack. "I think it stopped because it's run out."

Hugo nodded. "We should have been better prepared," he

said. "I knew that it would run out soon. I was more worried about what we were going to eat than thinking about the mission and rescuing Timmy."

"So was I," Henrietta said in a small voice. She was trembling.

"Chin up," said Hugo. "Now we must all put into practice everything we've learned as Christians. This is some storm!"

And he was right: it *was* some storm. With the first crash of thunder the rain began to fall. There was no way that they could put the cover back over the Rescue Craft in the storm and they had to endure the lashing rain, the flashing lightening and the crashing thunder as the shadows closed about them.

"What have we here?" a weird, thin voice spoke from the storm. They could not see it properly; there was only the glitter of eyes and the cold tones of the Snare.

"We're Christians," said Hugo.

"Christians heading for False Teaching?" taunted a different Snare.

"We're going to rescue a friend!" said Henrietta

There was the snigger of more Snares around them.

"The people in False Teaching belong to us!"

"Not if they want to be rescued," said Hugo.

There was a definite hesitation amongst the Snares.

"Has someone been praying for help?" they heard a Snare ask in horror.

"Silence!" demanded another, and Jack realised that the Snares had a leader with them, as they had the previous night. "These children know nothing! They're guessing!" said the nasty voice.

The problem was that they knew the Snare leader was right. They might be Christians; they had hastily put their armour on; they might have their Bibles in their hands; but they had not prepared for what might await them in the wilds of Err. They didn't have the right answers. They had not properly prepared to rescue Timmy. They really had no clue how to set about it.

Henrietta was rummaging in the Rescuer's Kit box. "We have prayers!" she said in sudden inspiration, remembering what Jack had told them about the effect that Mr Duffle's stick had on the Snares when they had captured Timmy, and remembering too Hezekiah's startling experiment with the prayer-stick in the dangerous drink.

"Prayers!" The concern of the Snares was evident as they muttered and debated amongst themselves.

"Silence!" the Snare leader hissed again. "These children know nothing about prayer or we could not have stopped them!"

Henrietta withdrew a stick from the Rescuer's Kit. "Look!" she said holding it high.

There was silence amongst the watching Snares.

And then Henrietta threw the stick at them with all her might.

They all held their breath as they watched the small stick of prayer fly through the air towards the Snares. There was a flare of light, as if someone had struck a match, a sudden sparkle... and then nothing at all. It was like a firework that had not really got started properly and had fizzled out. They looked at each other in dismay.

The Snares sniggered in amusement.

"What did I tell you?" said the big Snare leader, "they know nothing about prayer! They're no danger to us!"

"What do you want with us?" asked Hugo, raising his Bible above his head and dispelling the Snares that had crowded the closest to them with its light.

"What do we want with you?" taunted a Snare.

"With little Christians?" mocked another.

"You can't take us!" said Henrietta more boldly than she felt.

"Who said we wanted to?" the big leader Snare hissed at them.

"Then what do you want with us?" Hugo demanded again.

"Leave this place. It belongs to us!"

"But our friend…"

"Go!" hissed the big Snare. "And never come back!"

Hugo knew that they were defeated. They had no strategy to fight the storm of Snares around them. They did not know how to dispel them and get through the storm to rescue Timmy, wherever he was. They knew nothing about the work of a Rescuer. They were Christians and they had the basic tools, but they had no experience against these foes.

"We'll go," said Hugo.

"Hugo!" protested Henrietta. "There must be a way!" But even she was feeling defeated. If the prayer stick she had thrown didn't work, then what did? She had a hunch that if she just knew the right words from the Bible, it might drive them all away. She had learnt as much at school. But she had not paid enough attention and now the words would not come.

The rain began to cease and the sky lightened above them. They did not know the actual moment that the Snares melted away; they only felt the absence of their cold, oppressive presence.

"Do you want the last biscuit, Hugo?" Henrietta offered in a small voice. "I'm sorry I accused you about the muffins."

"That's okay, old thing," said Hugo. "You have it. Here, wrap yourself in this rug. I expect it'll warm up when the sun comes back out."

"We should have kept our helmets on all the time," said Hezekiah, "I expect we wouldn't have quarrelled then."

"Look!" Jack had picked up the Mission Detector and was gazing at the screen. Not only had the '*DANGER! SNARES!*' writing now disappeared, but under the name Timothy Trial at the top of the screen there was one word written in big, bold, white letters:

'*RESCUED!*'

CHAPTER 16
MR WEIGHTY TO THE RESCUE

They collected plenty of fuel for the Rescue Craft from the hedges and trees along the roadside and packed the fuel tank full of greenery. The sun came out and began to dry their wet clothes. Hugo suggested that they eat the remaining fruit and they put the apple cores and peach stones in the fuel tank too. They did not doubt that the Mission Detector was accurate and that somehow, miraculously, the rescue of Timmy had been accomplished. It just hadn't happened through them and now they were going to head home and face whatever consequences they must for their impulsive adventure.

Only one problem remained: the Rescue Craft still refused to start.

"I thought it stopped because it was low on fuel," said Jack, peering with Hugo into the fuel tank. Tufts of grass and leaves and twigs and a jumble of other things were packed to the very top of the tank. There was definitely enough fuel in it now.

"Perhaps I should drive," suggested Henrietta.

"And how exactly will you do that when we can't even start

the Craft?" retorted Hugo. "That's not your most sensible suggestion, Henry!"

Henrietta took it in good part. She was basking in the rays of the sun, glad to feel warm again. She was not going to get cross with Hugo now. Hezekiah sat with her on the settee (which had proved to be waterproof and was already dry) at the back of the Craft. He was also basking in the sun, happy that Hugo and Jack could solve their current problems, and more than content that they would soon be heading to Aletheia again.

"Perhaps the Detector machine can tell us why the Rescue Craft won't start," suggested Jack.

"Good idea!" said Henrietta. "You know, Hugo, Jack is really a lot smarter than you!"

"Jack was so brave last night," added Hezekiah.

"Good thinking, Jack," said Hugo, while Jack went a bit red at all their comments. "See if you can find out what's wrong on the Detector, Henry."

Henrietta began to press buttons. "It's got a whole section about the Rescue Craft Mechanics," she said. "Mr Weighty is pretty clever if he invented all this stuff! Let me see. I'll look under 'Starter Malfunction'. That sounds about right…"

"What does it say?" asked Hugo.

"Wait a minute, nearly there…ah ha! Code CD. Craft Disabled!"

"Disabled!" said Hugo in dismay. "I wonder what that means!"

"I think it means it won't start," said Henrietta.

"Well, actually that's the obvious bit, Henry," said Hugo.

Hezekiah giggled faintly.

"Someone's coming," said Jack. "They might be able to help."

It seemed too good to be true that anyone would help them in this part of Err. After their experience with Wander Palm, and knowing that the people they were likely to meet here would not necessarily be 'on their side', all three of them looked warily down the road towards False Teaching at the two figures that were coming their way. Were they friends or were they foes? At least it wasn't more Snares, for the figures were those of a big man and a tall boy. They were definitely interested in the Rescue Craft though; they were pointing their way.

Henrietta, with her sharp eyes, was the first to discover the identity of the newcomers. "It's Barmy!" she shrieked. "And Mr Weighty with him!" and she set off running down the road towards them.

Hugo watched her go. He was pleased, of course. He was very pleased that help was at hand and that they were at last reunited with Timmy. But now they must face the consequences of everything that they had done when they took things into their own hands and set off to rescue the three boys. And they must face Mr Weighty whose wonderful Rescue Craft they had so impulsively 'borrowed': and which now lay broken by the side of the road in the middle of Err.

Mr Weighty greeted them all like old friends, not naughty children; he really was a very nice man. There was some initial chaos while greetings were exchanged and Hugo and Henrietta offered red-faced apologies, and then Mr Weighty opened the enormous rucksack he carried on his back and distributed large sandwiches of many varieties – ham and cheese and pickle and eggs and sausages and more besides. He also gave them cool, refreshing Water of Sound Doctrine to drink, and a wonderful toffee cake, specially sealed to keep it from decaying in the air of Err. He didn't scold Hugo and Henrietta for taking his Rescue Craft without permission; he merely said that there would be plenty of 'others' that would point out the error of their ways without him adding to their burdens.

Hugo and Henrietta were well aware of those 'others' of course. Their father and mother and their school teachers too would have plenty to say about their foolhardy adventure and they were exceedingly grateful to Mr Weighty for not punishing or lecturing them for what they had done.

"We thought we could manage to rescue Barmy on our own," said Henrietta.

"I think Mr Weighty knows that now, Henry," said Hugo.

Mr Weighty chuckled. "And now what do you think?" he asked.

"Well, we didn't really know how to rescue Barmy," said Henrietta.

"It takes experience as a Christian and a Rescuer to be properly prepared to go into enemy territory and rescue others," said Mr Weighty. "There are many enemies and many other dangers that you know nothing about. If you've learned anything from your adventure let it be that you need to rely more on God to show you how to grow as a Christian, and less on your own ideas about what you should do!"

"Thanks for trying to rescue me though," said Timmy. "I mean," he turned to Mr Weighty, "I know they weren't right," he said, "but it was pretty good of them to try and find me, wasn't it?"

Mr Weighty smiled. "You have good friends with good intentions, Timmy," he agreed. "But of course you know now that God was always seeking you and longing to save you[11]. He would never have left you long without help once you started to cry for help to Him."

Hugo and Henrietta, Jack and Hezekiah stared at Timmy who sat with them in the sunshine on the rug that Mr Weighty had spread over the now dry grass for them to have their picnic. He was Timmy, and yet he was not.

"Are you a Christian now, Barmy?" Hezekiah asked in awe.

Timmy no longer seemed to mind the 'barmy' tag from Hezekiah. "Yes," he said. "I know now that I wasn't before, but now…" and his eyes filled with tears that the others pretended not to see, "now the Lord Jesus has saved me. Now I know what it means to be a Christian."

Henrietta dashed away a tear from her eye. "I'm so glad, Barmy," she said, "so glad!"

Hugo cleared his throat.

Jack was too incredulous to speak at all but it was to him that Timmy turned first.

"I'm sorry," Timmy said awkwardly, "for everything. I know I've been pretty bad to you lot too," he said, glancing at Hezekiah in particular, "but Jack knows how awful I've been back at home and at school."

"That's alright," stuttered Jack. "It's fine now."

Mr Weighty clapped Timmy on the back. "A fine start, son," he said. "It's a fine start to Christian life when you set out to put right your wrongs! It would be good if we could all remember to do that every day of our lives!"

It did not take long for Mr Weighty to 'fix' the malfunction of the Rescue Craft. To their astonishment it transpired that Mr Weighty himself had disabled the Rescue Craft with a remote control which was one of his particularly clever inventions "even if I say so myself!" he said. "The remote control overrides anything anyone else is doing in the Craft. I could even have made it come home again if I wanted to!"

"Then, you could have stopped us at any time!" gasped Henrietta. "You could have stopped us right away!"

"Yes," said Mr Weighty. "I certainly could have."

"But why?" asked Hugo. "Why didn't you just take over and bring us back?"

"You make your own choices, my boy," said Mr Weighty. "Sometimes you have to learn your lessons the hard way. But I was watching out for you. I wouldn't have let any harm come to you, I assured your brother Harold of that! I could see your location at every moment on my Master Controller."

"Where's Harold?" asked Hugo.

"He should be at my house when we stop there for tea," said Mr Weighty. "Then he'll take you all home to Aletheia with him."

Hugo and Henrietta were silent. It was the thought of facing their oldest brother Harold with the account of their doomed expedition. Harold was training to be a Rescuer and they greatly admired him. They had just never realised how much there was to his work. But face Harold they must, and very soon they were all seated in the Rescue Craft, Hugo and Timmy in the front with Mr Weighty, and Henrietta, Hezekiah and Jack sharing the settee at the back. They clutched onto the sides as Mr Weighty went speeding around the bends and flying down the straights. They were going towards Aletheia once more.

They had plenty of questions of course, and they talked for most of that return journey. How could they have defeated the

Snares? What verses from the Bible might have stopped the Snares? How did Mr Weighty find Timmy? How did he rescue him on his own against all those Snares? Why didn't the stick, which was the prayer weapon Henrietta found in the Rescuer's Kit, work when they tried it on the Snares?

"We tried one of your prayer sticks against the Snares you see," Hugo explained to Mr Weighty.

"I threw it at them," said Henrietta in a small voice.

"But why didn't it work?" asked Hugo.

"My dear Hugo," said Mr Weighty, "you might have been throwing prayers for the Lost Ones in the Mountains of Destruction at the Snares of False Teaching! Those prayers have got nothing to do with them! Come to think of it, I did have some prayers collected for Mr Faintnot who is the Outpost Rescuer up near the Mountains of Destruction. I was going to deliver the prayers to him. I think it's prayers for poor Mr Faintnot that you've been throwing at the Snares!"

"It was only one," said Henrietta, looking thoroughly ashamed.

"Well, it's done now," said Mr Weighty, "but since the Snares you met are focussed on keeping people in False Teaching, prayer for people in the Mountains of Destruction wouldn't have had much effect on them! You have to be specific and targeted in prayer. You can't just expect to aim any prayer at any problem and get results. One of the secrets of effective prayer is praying specifically like Elijah did in the Bible[7]. Mr Duffle's sticks worked wonderfully for Timmy and Jack because he had given the sticks to them; he was praying for them. One of the keys to a successful mission is preparing with prayer and asking people to provide prayer cover that is specific to the problems you're going to face."

"I see," said Hugo.

"I think we have a lot to learn," said Henrietta.

"I think we already know that, Henry," said Hugo.

Mr Weighty smiled. "Perhaps you know more than you think," he said kindly. "Think about the truth of Redemption. You know that when the Lord Jesus died, He paid the ransom[12] for the sins of the whole world. But not everyone will be saved. Just as Timmy did recently, people have to choose to accept the payment that the Lord Jesus made on their behalf, and then they are set free from paying the penalty for their sins themselves. Ultimately, the process of redemption is complete when the Lord Jesus takes us home to heaven, and then we are claimed completely by Him."

"Yes," said Hugo, "we learned a bit about that at school,

remember, Henry? Redemption is being purchased by God instead of being owned by sin; being set free from sin to belong to God instead."

Henrietta simply nodded. She wished she had paid more attention to the Bible teaching at school. She had trusted in the Lord Jesus and was saved, but she had never really thought how vital these details would be when they faced real enemies and real dangers in the land of Err.

"That's good, Hugo," said Mr Weighty.

"Can the Lord Jesus set anyone free from anything? I mean, people who have been really, really bad?" asked Hezekiah.

"Absolutely," said Mr Weighty. "There is no sin or wrong that has not been already paid for by the Lord Jesus! There is no one too bad to be saved. In fact, the worst sinner has already been saved!"

"Oh, I know who that was," said Hezekiah. "The Apostle Paul![13]"

"Very good!" said Mr Weighty. "So, you do listen at school sometimes!"

"So, what happens to someone who isn't a Christian who gets taken by Snares?" asked Jack, trying not to look at Timmy too much. "How do they get free?" he still found it amazing that Timmy was really and truly there, safe and sound and somehow miraculously extracted from all those awful Snares.

"Well, it's like it was with Timmy," said Mr Weighty. "When Timmy cried out to God to save him and set him free from the Snares of sin that had a hold of him, then they no longer had any authority over him."

"Did the Snares just let go?" asked Hezekiah.

Mr Weighty nodded. "They had to," he said. "Because the Lord Jesus paid the price to set Timmy free; and when Timmy turned to Him and asked to be set free, the price the Lord Jesus paid is put to Timmy's account."

"Wow," said Hezekiah.

"It's the same with anyone who gets saved," said Mr Weighty. "It happened to all of you too when you trusted in the Lord Jesus. We are all snared by sin. We might not have got taken captive quite like Timmy, but we all needed to be set free. And that's what happens when we simply trust in the Lord Jesus."

"So, it's up to the person who's been captured to want to be set free?"

"Yes," Mr Weighty said. "If they continue in sin and don't

want God in their life then of course the Snares can hold them captive. But the moment a person asks to be set free and relies on what the Lord Jesus has done then the victory is won! It's partly why I wanted to wait until the morning to go after Timmy," Mr Weighty added. "You see, I knew that there could be no rescue unless Timmy himself wanted to be set free."

"Oh," said Henrietta. "We didn't know that either."

"We won't get lost in Err again," said Hugo earnestly.

But when he glanced at Mr Weighty, it seemed that Mr Weighty was faintly smiling and there was a twinkle in his eye when he said, "I wonder…"

Timmy said the least on that journey back to the Weightys' home on Apathy Road. He was pale and worn and kept his eyes fixed unwaveringly ahead of him as if he never wanted to look away again.

"What are you thinking, Barmy?" asked Henrietta.

"I'm just looking at the cross," said Timmy. "I'm thinking about how much it cost the Lord Jesus to set me free."

And a tear fell down his cheek.

CHAPTER 17
BACK TO ALETHEIA

The Weightys' home on Apathy Road was a Rescuer Outpost. It was a centre of safety and calm in the midst of the Snares and other creatures and pitfalls of Err. The house was like the Weightys themselves: big and solid and sturdy and inviting. It was colourful too. Even as the evening darkness closed in and the mist once more descended the windows shone with a bright, welcoming light and the coloured fairy lights around the edges of the big house made it look a bit like Christmas. There were even twinkling lights around the tall turret at the very top of the house.

"That's our prayer tower," explained Mr Weighty. "It has a great view of the cross!"

Mr Weighty parked the Rescue Craft in his shed and ushered them all towards his home.

"I think I'll fit a lock on my shed," he said mischievously, "it might save others from the temptation of taking my Rescue Craft!"

Hugo and Henrietta looked ashamed all over again.

"Never mind," said Mr Weighty. "I'm only pulling your leg!"

Mrs Weighty met them all at the door, and if they had thought that she might receive them as naughty children and not as treasured guests they were happily mistaken. She said nothing about Hugo and Henrietta raiding her kitchen for food for their trip. She didn't mention them taking the Rescue Craft away so that Mr Weighty was even without his own transport for his mission to rescue Timmy. She didn't even comment on the dishevelled state of their clothes. She gave them all a welcoming hug and took them into the lovely cosy dining room where a big fire was crackling cheerfully in the fireplace. A large table laden with food stood before the fire, and standing by the fire there was also a young man who looked pretty stern. It was Harold Wallop.

Henrietta and Hugo hung back, looking at each other and at their grim faced eldest sibling. Harold greeted the others warmly, and then he turned to the twins.

"I suppose you two realise the trouble you've caused," he said.

"Yes," said Henrietta. "I promise we do. So there's probably no need to say lots about it."

"I think that's wishful thinking, Henry," said Hugo.

"You could say that," said Harold.

Mrs Weighty came to the rescue. "Tea's ready!" she said.

It was a wonderful meal. There was cheese on toast and pizza and scrambled eggs and hot sausages and stacks of bread and butter and half a dozen types of jam and the most enormous sponge cake and cream.

"Wow!" said Hugo, cheering up despite Harold's worrying expression. "And there are more of those chocolate muffins too, Henry!"

"Oh," said Mrs Weighty with a twinkle in her eyes, "you liked those muffins, did you?"

Hugo immediately looked embarrassed. "I'm sorry we took them," he said.

"That's water under the bridge," said Mrs Weighty. "I was only teasing."

"You took food from Mrs Weighty too?" asked Harold incredulously.

"Bad timing, Hugo," said Henrietta. "We could have talked about all that *after* tea." She feared that she might lose out on the wonderful feast all ready to be consumed.

Harold looked like he might choke on his pizza. "You really are the limit!" he began.

"We do know that," said Henrietta, "honestly we do…"

"I took food from the Wallops' house too," said Timmy, looking at Hezekiah.

Henrietta stared at Timmy. "I was going to punch you for that," she said, "but I guess what we've done is even worse!"

"I'm glad you think so," said Harold drily.

"We do," said Henrietta earnestly.

Hugo kicked her under the table. "Don't keep saying things," he hissed at her.

"It was really all my fault anyway," said Timmy. "I shouldn't have gone away from Aletheia."

They all looked at him. It still took some getting used to, the dramatic change in Timmy.

"It's true," he said. "And I'm sorry."

"You can't say fairer than that," said Mr Weighty. "You're a brave man to admit your failings and apologise, Timmy, very brave!"

"Lots of it was our fault too," said Henrietta.

Hugo aimed another kick at her under the table but she had tucked her legs well out of the way and ignored him. Hugo sighed at his exasperating twin and applied himself to his food.

"You wouldn't have come after me if I hadn't run away," said Timmy.

"That's very good of you, Timmy," said Harold, "but I can assure you that Hugo and Henry have their own way of landing in trouble without your encouragement!"

"But we know some things about rescuing people that we didn't know before," said Henrietta.

Hugo aimed yet another kick and managed to reach her. She glared at him.

"Mr Weighty explained some things to us," said Hezekiah, sticking up for his sister.

"Not enough, however," said Mr Weighty, "to launch another rescue mission of your own!"

"Oh no," said Henrietta, "of course not!"

"With the right call for help, and the right armour, and the right weapon and the right prayer support, anything is possible," said Mr Weighty. "You need training and experience in Christian life to know how to manage these things. You'll understand more the more you study the Bible."

"Would Bible verses have helped us against the Snares?" asked Henrietta.

"The Word of God is always helpful," said Mr Weighty, "but you must learn to use it right. You must learn verses from the Bible and hide them in your heart to keep yourself right[14] so that you know what to say. And you shouldn't just pick a random verse or take a verse out of its proper context and expect it to have the full impact of the living and powerful Word of God[15]. You must learn to use it wisely."

Henrietta sighed. It all made so much sense when Mr Weighty explained it to them, but they had so much more to learn.

It was dark when they left the Weightys' cosy house and set off through the chilly mist up Apathy Road to Aletheia. Harold wasn't being cross with the twins anymore. He saw how sorry they were and knew that they were in for a hard time when they reached home and faced their parents and then their school teachers at school the next day. "You'd better get it over with," he sympathised. "It's never quite as bad as you think it will be."

"It probably is," said Henrietta sadly.

She and Hugo were resigned to their fate. And at least they had the comfort that, whatever punishments they might face, they would face them together.

Mr Weighty offered to lend them his Rescue Craft for the final part of the return journey to Aletheia but Harold thought that they would all manage the long walk back up the hill despite their weariness. Henrietta would dearly have loved to travel in the Rescue Craft but she did not dare to say so. Jack would like to have driven it once more and Hugo wanted to have another look at the Mission Detector to see if he could detect anyone praying for help. They said these things quietly to each other as they strapped on their armour. Timmy put on the pieces of the armour that Mr Weighty provided for him. At last he could see the armour of God that the others had talked about and that he had scorned; and he put on his armour as if it was the greatest honour in the world.

That weary walk through the darkness of Err was nothing like the wandering of the night before. They were not lost or full of fear or doubts: because they could always see the cross before them and besides, they had Harold as their guide. They held their Bibles in their hands for light and only occasionally commented about the fact that they were no longer travelling in Mr Weighty's wonderful Rescue Craft.

Timmy didn't comment at all.

He walked with his eyes fixed on the cross.

Redemption Square was deserted when at last they reached the top of the long hill of the city of Aletheia and stood near the cross. A few of the windows of the shops and houses clustered around the square twinkled with light but everyone was indoors and most people had already gone to bed. Harold led them to the cross and they climbed the steps to the top, to the very foot of the cross, and looked out over the whole land of Err.

"It's the best view in the land," said Harold. "Best because you can see the most, and also because you can feel the most. Here you can feel the right amount of compassion and anxiety and even righteous anger about Err, because you're close to the cross."

It was dark and the air was cool and clear. Millions of stars twinkled above them and the moon was high in the sky. In the South, the way they had all gone to Wishy-Washy Fair and beyond, the air was hazy and the view grew dim. They could all remember the damp, chilling mist of night and how it obscured and confused everything around. But somewhere in that mist the Weightys' sturdy, colourful home stood ready to reach the people around them with the message of the Truth of the Bible about how people could be set free from their sin. Even now, Mr and Mrs Weighty might be in their prayer tower, looking through their big window in the direction of the cross where the children stood with Harold.

In the other direction, in the North, the stars shone brightly but in the distance cruel storm clouds gathered and blackened the night sky. The dim shape of huge mountains could be seen and around and about them there seemed to be an ominous red glow, as if there was a huge fire somewhere there. One of the mountains even looked like a volcano.

"Are there really monsters in the North?" asked Jack.

Harold looked a bit grim. "There are awful things there," he said.

"What *is* there?" asked Timmy.

"Things you'll learn about when you're ready to," said Harold.

"I'd like to go and rescue people from there one day," said Hugo.

"I think I *must* go sometime," said Henrietta. "I wasted that precious prayer for the people near the Mountains of

Destruction, remember?"

"Then *you* must all remember to pray," said Harold.

They walked the remaining short distance through the dark, narrow streets of Aletheia and to the Wallops' apartment at last. They were footsore and weary as they entered the Foundation-of-Faith Apartment block and Harold said that they could all take the elevator to the top floor. Timmy was surprised to find that there was a lift contraption after all.

It was an old fashioned elevator with doors you pulled shut and fastened, with cushioned seats around the walls, and with a thick carpet on the floor. How it was powered wasn't clear, but there was an indicator on the wall outside of the elevator which showed how much power it currently had and how far it could take you. '*All the way to the top*' was the current reading on the indicator.

"That's good," said Hezekiah wearily. "We won't have to climb any stairs!"

"I think I'll fall asleep on the way to the top," admitted Henrietta. She stepped inside the elevator and sank down on one of the cushioned seats. "Come on, Zek," she said, and patted the seat beside her.

Hugo followed Hezekiah into the contraption and Jack looked into the curiously comfortable interior. It was difficult to see how big, or how small, the elevator was but there was still plenty of room inside.

Harold followed his brothers and sister into the elevator and looked back at the two boys. "Coming?" he asked.

Timmy went next and then Jack.

And walking through that elevator door was perhaps the strangest feeling yet of their very strange adventure.

CHAPTER 18
HOME AT LAST

When Jack walked through the elevator door he shut his eyes tightly against the sudden brightness of the light. When he opened his eyes he realised that the glaring light was the hot sun which was shining brightly in the sky above him. Timmy stood close by, and both boys looked around them, and then stared at each other in silence.

Behind them were the farm sheds that belonged to Jack's Grandad; before them stretched the field of golden barley waving and nodding in the warm summer breeze; and from behind the sheds came the sound of children playing in a playground.

Was it possible that it was still only Friday lunchtime? Was it possible that they hadn't been missed at all? Had everything been an incredible dream? Jack looked at Timmy. Timmy looked at Jack. And Jack knew that if he looked anything like Timmy, his school uniform dirty, his hair wild, his face pale, and even a bruise on his forehead: well then, they must have been somewhere!

They began to make a careful examination of the farm sheds.

They were both padlocked and silent and without any sign that they were remotely inhabited. Jack removed his spy watch from his pocket. He remembered the last time that he had looked at it, when he was lost in the land of Err. And as he looked at it now, with tall, untidy, stained Timmy looking over his shoulder, they saw the words *'True Aletheia Time: Time to go home!'* fading slowly from the screen.

Timmy smiled. "I was afraid it was all a dream," he said.

Jack grinned in return. "But you're different," he said. "It must be true!"

For, while they might be in doubt about many of the things that had happened that Friday lunchtime, one thing was beyond dispute, and that was that Timmy Trial had changed. Apart from the wild appearance of the two boys, which certainly proved that *something* had happened, there was a remarkable difference in Timmy. There was only one possible explanation: Timmy had become a Christian.

Jack and Timmy heard the school bell sound the end of lunchtime and they both set off at a jog around the sheds and back to the gap in the hedge that led to the school grounds.

"If there's any trouble," said Timmy, "I'm going to tell them that it was my fault that you left the school grounds. I chased you out of school."

"That's Ok," said Jack. "It's probably nothing to what Hugo and Henrietta are going to face!"

Timmy laughed. It was a strange thought that their friends, in an unknown land far away, were also facing punishment for the same strange events.

But, apart from the indignation of their teachers and their parents about the state of their clothes and general appearance, the boys faced very little questioning over that lunchtime escapade. It was assumed by their friends that they had been fighting; but both Jack and Timmy denied all knowledge of that. And besides, there was no doubt that they had returned from their excursion outside of the school grounds the very best of friends.

There were perhaps only two more immediate consequences of the adventure for Jack.

The first was that Jack astounded his teacher, Mrs Bubble, by offering to re-do his maths questions.

"I didn't do them right, you see," he told her. "And although I probably won't get them right if I do them again, I'll make sure I try properly this time."

A bemused Mrs Bubble returned Jack's exercise book to him, thinking, not for the first time, that teaching was never likely to be dull while she had Jack Merryweather in her class. And Jack diligently spent some time on Saturday re-doing his maths questions because he thought it would be pleasing to the Lord Jesus if he truly tried his best.

The second consequence of the adventure was that Jack could never adequately explain the complete disappearance of his school rucksack. No amount of diligent searching ever revealed its hiding place – which of course Jack well knew. He had last seen it in Mr and Mrs Weighty's stall at Wishy-Washy Fair. He sincerely hoped that they had made good use of his lunchtime sandwiches which had been his favourites; he wondered whether they had ever tasted marmite in Err before.

Jack and Timmy often discussed their Aletheian adventure

and the things that had happened to each of them, including when they were apart.

"I wonder what would have happened if you had met Wonky Dollar at Wishy-Washy Fair and gone with him to the Academy of Science-Explains-All with that piece of lego," mused Jack.

"That lego!" exclaimed Timmy. "That was a pretty strange bit of the story, wasn't it?"

"I wonder if they've found out by now that it was made in 2005," said Jack. He had checked the lego box when he returned. Made in 2005 was a very long way from the millions of years old that the scientists in Err thought the lego might be.

"I wonder what year it is in Aletheia anyway," responded Timmy.

Jack knew he was thinking about their friends in Aletheia. Were they growing older at the same rate as Jack and Timmy were, or were they far ahead already? Had they lived years in the weeks since their strange adventure? Jack wondered whether Timmy also thought about Henrietta Wallop. But he didn't ask.

"If you had found Wonky Dollar at the Fair," said Jack, "then you might never have been taken by Snares. You might have travelled with him in one of those strange big caravans we saw, or perhaps in an Atob, and got safely back to Alternative Teaching and bumped into us again!"

Timmy immediately looked serious. "If I had never been taken by Snares," he said, "then I don't know if I would have trusted in the Lord Jesus. I needed to be taken…because that helped me to realise how much I needed to be saved."

"I wonder if that's why it all happened that way," mused Jack.

"I'm glad it did," said Timmy.

They often discussed the challenges of Christian life too. It was a natural consequence of the lessons that they had learned so vividly in Aletheia that they should try to put them into practice, even in their quiet village in England. They went to the local church regularly where the Bible was taught, and they talked to their understanding Sunday School teacher about some of the things they puzzled over. They came to understand a little more about how they should be wearing their Christian armour of God[5] every day.

The helmet of salvation was the mind, and they needed to train and guard and keep their minds focussed on the salvation that God had provided for them and what the Lord Jesus had done when he paid the price for the sins of the whole world[12];

The breastplate – or body armour – of righteousness guarded the most vulnerable part of a person: it guarded behind them where they couldn't see, and the front of them where the feelings of a person were in the heart. And so they must always guard their heart and feelings against desiring wrong things.

The belt of truth meant that they must be always surrounded and held together by the whole Truth of the Bible, not diluting it or changing it in any way.

Their feet were the only part of them constantly touching the world and on their feet they must wear their gospel boots: they must always be prepared to go to people who weren't saved and bring them the gospel of peace which was the good news about the Lord Jesus.

The shield of faith meant that, if they were suddenly attacked and made to doubt that what God said was right and true, they must learn to always have faith in God and His Word the Bible.

And their only, their most vital weapon, was the Bible itself and all that it contained. It was the living and powerful Word of God[15] so they must study it, learn it, use it in context in the right way, and rely only on what God said. Only then could they gain the victory in the battle of the small things of everyday life and in the big decisions that they might one day face.

And always, every day, around and about their entire lives, was the invisible, mighty power of prayer. At any moment they had access to God in Heaven who would hear them; and God could do anything.

"Do you think we'll ever go back to Aletheia?" Timmy asked Jack wistfully from time to time.

"I hope so," Jack always replied.

Bible References

Unless otherwise stated, all references are taken from the New King James Version of the Bible.

1. There is a verse in the Bible which is about doing everything for the glory of God. This is found in **1 Corinthians 10:31**:
    "Therefore, whether you eat or drink, or whatever you do, do all to the glory of God."

2. There are many verses in the Bible that explain how to become a Christian. Here are some examples:

    John 3:16:
    "For God so loved the world that He gave His only begotten Son, that whoever believes in Him should not perish but have everlasting life."

    Acts 16:31:
    "Believe on the Lord Jesus Christ, and you will be saved…"

    Romans 10:9:
    "That if you confess with your mouth the Lord Jesus and believe in your heart that God has raised Him from the dead, you will be saved."

3. 'Sin' is the Bible name for all the wrong that people do against God. The Bible teaches that everyone has sinned against God. This can be found in **Romans 3:23**:
    "For all have sinned and fall short of the glory of God."

4. This is a reference to **Proverbs 23:5**:

    "Will you set your heart on that which is not?
    For riches certainly make themselves wings;
    They fly like an eagle toward heaven."

    [The Bible does not mean that money literally flies; this verse is saying that riches are easily lost.]

5. The Bible talks about the Christian putting on the 'armour of God'. This is explained in **Ephesians 6:10-18**:

    "Finally, my brethren, be strong in the Lord and in the power of His might.
    Put on the whole armour of God, that you may be able to stand against the wiles of the devil. For we do not wrestle against flesh and blood, but against principalities, against powers, against the rulers of the darkness of this age, against spiritual hosts of wickedness in the heavenly place. Therefore take up the whole armour of God, that you may be able to withstand in the evil day, and having done all, to stand.
    Stand therefore, having girded your waist with truth, having put on the breastplate of righteousness, and having shod your feet with the preparation of the gospel of peace; above all, taking the shield of faith with which you will be able to quench all the fiery darts of the wicked one. And take the helmet of salvation, and the sword of the Spirit, which is the word of God; praying always with all prayer and supplication in the Spirit..."

6. In **Ephesians 6:17** the Bible is described as *"the sword of the Spirit which is the Word of God."*

7. This quote from **James 5:16-18** which explains about effective prayer:
    "…The effective, fervent prayer of a righteous man avails much.
    Elijah was a man with a nature like ours, and he prayed earnestly that
    it would not rain; and it did not rain on the land for three years and six
    months.
    And he prayed again, and the heaven gave rain, and the earth produced
    its fruit."

8. This is a reference to a verse in **Psalm 119:105** which explains how the
    Bible can show us the way:
    "Your word is a lamp to my feet
    And a light to my path"

9. You can read about the promise of the Lord Jesus to send another Help-
    er (or Comforter) to Christians in **John 14:16-17** (see below). This is
    the Holy Spirit who is a Divine Person who helps and guides Christians
    today.
    "And I will pray the Father, and He will give you another Helper, that He
    may abide with you forever – the Spirit of truth, whom the world cannot
    receive…"

10. You can read the account of how God made the world in the book of
    Genesis, chapter 1.

11. The Bible makes it clear that the Lord Jesus came to seek and save
    people. You can read a verse about this in **Luke 19:10**:
    "For the Son of Man has come to seek and to save that which was lost."

12. The Bible describes the Lord Jesus as giving Himself as a "ransom" –
that is paying the price – for all those who trust in Him. Examples of
verses about the Lord Jesus being a ransom are:

Matthew 20:28:

*"Just as the Son of Man did not come to be served, but to serve, and to
give His life a ransom for many."*

1 Timothy 2:5-6:

*"For there is one God and one Mediator between God and men, the
Man Christ Jesus, who gave Himself a ransom for all, to be testified in
due time."*

13. This is a reference to a verse in the Bible in which the Apostle Paul
describes himself as the chief of sinners. This can be found in **1
Timothy 1:15**:

*"This is a faithful saying and worthy of all acceptation, that Christ Jesus
came into the world to save sinners, of whom I am the chief."*

14. This is a reference to **Psalm 119:11**:

*"Your word have I hidden in my heart,
That I might not sin against You."*

15. This is a reference to **Hebrews 4:12**:

*"For the word of God is living and powerful, and sharper than any two-
edged sword, piercing even to the division of soul and spirit, and of joints
and marrow, and is a discerner of the thoughts and intents of the heart."*